HANDS-ON ZIG PROGRAMMING

A Practical Guide to Building Real-World Systems Applications for Developers

Paul G. Julius

Table of Content

PREFACE...5

Part 1: GETTING STARTED WITH ZIG.......................................10
1. Introduction to Zig...11
   Overview of Zig...12
   Features and use cases..14
2. Setting Up Your Development Environment.................15
   Installing Zig...16
   IDEs, tools, and configuration.......................................17
3. Zig Basics..21
   Syntax, variables, and data types..................................21
   Functions and control flow..23
   Error handling and testing basics.................................26

Part 2: CORE CONCEPTS AND LANGUAGE FEATURES.........29
4. Memory Management in Zig..34
   Manual memory management principles.......................34
   Allocators and deallocators..36
5. Error Handling and Safety...43
   Zig's approach to errors..43
   Error unions and catch patterns...................................46
6. Concurrency and Asynchronous Programming.............51
   Using async/await...52
   Building lightweight concurrency models.....................54
7. Working with Types 59
   Structs, enums, and unions...59
   Generics and type inference..65

Part 3: BUILDING REAL-WORLD APPLICATIONS 69

8. Building a CLI Application 72

Parsing arguments 73

Interacting with files and the OS 75

9. Developing a Networking Application 83

Sockets and protocols 83

Handling concurrency in networked systems 86

10. Creating a High-Performance Library 95

Optimizing for speed and memory efficiency 95

Writing reusable modules 98

11. Interfacing with C and Other Languages 104

Interop with C libraries 104

FFI principles 107

12. Zig for Systems Programming 113

Bare-metal programming basics 113

Writing a custom allocator 116

13. Debugging and Profiling Zig Applications 123

Debugging tools and techniques 123

Profiling and performance tuning 125

14. Writing Cross-Platform Code 133

Handling platform differences 133

Conditional compilation 136

15. Contributing to Zig Projects 144

Zig ecosystem overview 144

Best practices for contributing 147

Part 4: CASE STUDIES AND NEXT STEPS 151

16. Case Study: Building a Complete Application 154

End-to-end example project 154

17. The Zig Ecosystem and Community 161

Exploring Zig libraries and tools 161

Staying updated with Zig's development..164

CONCLUSION...168

Preface

Welcome to Hands-On Zig Programming: A Practical Guide to Building Real-World Systems Applications for Developers*. Whether you're an experienced programmer exploring a new language or a curious newcomer venturing into systems programming, this book is crafted to guide you on an exciting journey with Zig—a language that combines simplicity, control, and performance in ways that few others can match.

In an era dominated by high-level abstractions and bloated libraries, many developers have felt the increasing disconnect between their code and the hardware it runs on. We rely on complex tools to manage memory, handle errors, and optimize performance, often sacrificing control for convenience. But what if there was a language that could bridge the gap between the raw power of systems programming and the ease of high-level development? Enter Zig.

Why Zig?
Zig is not just another programming language; it's a philosophy. Built with simplicity and explicitness at its core, Zig enables developers to write efficient, predictable, and highly portable code. It strips away unnecessary abstractions and gives you the tools to manage complexity without losing control. Zig doesn't try to shield you from the realities of the machine; instead, it equips you with the clarity to face them head-on.

This philosophy makes Zig an excellent choice for developers who are serious about systems programming, but its benefits don't stop there. Whether you're building an operating system, creating a high-performance library, or crafting a lightweight web server, Zig offers a robust yet approachable foundation for solving real-world problems.

Who Should Read This Book?

This book is designed for developers seeking a clear and accessible introduction to systems programming. It covers key concepts like memory management, error handling, and performance optimization, all while guiding you in building practical, real-world applications. You'll also learn how to write high-quality, maintainable, and portable code using Zig, a modern programming language. Whether your background is in low-level languages like C, C++, or Rust, or high-level languages like Python or JavaScript, Zig offers a refreshing blend of modern features and the foundational principles of programming.

What Makes This Book Unique?

When designing this book, we focused on three guiding principles:

1. Practicality: This isn't just a language reference or a collection of syntax rules. Each chapter dives into hands-on examples, projects, and exercises that show you how Zig can solve real-world problems. From building CLI tools to networking applications, we cover a wide range of use cases.

2. Clarity: Zig's simplicity is one of its greatest strengths, and we aim to reflect that in our explanations. Complex topics like memory management, concurrency, and interfacing with C are broken down into digestible steps.

3. Relevance: Zig is a language for today's developers. It embraces modern paradigms while staying rooted in the foundational principles of programming. This book highlights Zig's role in the evolving world of software development and systems programming.

What You'll Learn

By the time you finish this book, you'll not only have a solid understanding of Zig's features but also the confidence to apply them in your own projects. Here's a glimpse of what's ahead:

- Foundations of Zig: We'll start with the basics—syntax, types, control flow, and functions. This will set the stage for more advanced topics.
- Memory and Safety: Learn how to manage memory explicitly, write safe and robust code, and leverage Zig's unique error-handling model.
- Concurrency and Performance: Discover how to build efficient, multi-threaded applications without the complexity often associated with low-level programming.
- Real-World Applications: From command-line tools to networked systems, we'll walk through practical examples that you can adapt to your own needs.
- Interfacing with C: Harness the power of Zig's interoperability to use existing C libraries or gradually migrate legacy projects to Zig.
- Advanced Systems Programming: For those ready to go deeper, we'll explore writing custom allocators, debugging, and profiling Zig applications.

Each chapter builds on the previous one, ensuring that you're never left guessing. By the end, you'll have a complete understanding of how to leverage Zig to build robust and efficient software.

Why This Book Matters

The software industry is evolving rapidly. While high-level languages have enabled a surge in productivity and innovation, they've also led to a sense of detachment from the underlying hardware. Zig offers a chance to reconnect with the fundamentals. It reminds us that great software isn't just about delivering functionality; it's about delivering functionality with precision, efficiency, and elegance. More importantly, Zig represents a paradigm shift in how we think about systems programming. It challenges the idea that low-level programming has to be cryptic or error-prone. Instead, Zig combines the power of languages like C with the modern features and safety guarantees that developers expect in 21st-century software.

A Personal Note
I discovered Zig during a period of frustration. Despite years of experience in programming, I often found myself wrestling with languages that either felt too cumbersome or too opaque. Zig was like a breath of fresh air—simple, intuitive, and unapologetically focused on empowering the developer.

As I dug deeper, I realized that Zig wasn't just a tool; it was a mindset. It encouraged me to write better code, think more critically about design decisions, and appreciate the balance between control and simplicity. My hope is that this book will inspire you in the same way.

How to Use This Book
This book is meant to be both a guide and a companion. You can read it cover to cover, or you can jump to the chapters that interest you most. Each chapter includes practical exercises and code examples that you can follow along with. Don't be afraid to experiment—Zig is a language that rewards curiosity. I also encourage you to join the growing Zig community. There's a vibrant ecosystem of developers who are eager to share knowledge, discuss ideas, and help newcomers. By contributing

to this community, you'll not only deepen your understanding of Zig but also play a part in shaping its future.

Programming is more than just writing code—it's about solving problems, exploring possibilities, and creating tools that make a difference. Zig embodies these principles, and I believe it has the potential to redefine how we think about systems programming.

This book is an invitation to embark on that journey. It's an opportunity to learn, grow, and discover what's possible when you combine the power of Zig with your own creativity and ingenuity.

Part 1:

GETTING STARTED WITH ZIG

AN INTRODUCTION

Zig is an emerging programming language designed with a focus on simplicity, performance, and reliability. It stands out as a modern alternative for systems programming while embracing the essential principles that have shaped the field. Whether you're coming from a background in low-level programming with languages like C or Rust, or transitioning from higher-level languages such as Python or JavaScript, Zig offers an intuitive yet powerful approach to tackling software development challenges.

Part 1 of this book, *Getting Started with Zig*, introduces the fundamental concepts and tools you'll need to write your first Zig programs. It lays the groundwork for understanding the language's unique philosophy and prepares you to explore its potential for building efficient and maintainable systems.

Before diving into the technical details, it's important to understand what makes Zig a compelling choice for developers. At its core, Zig emphasizes three key principles: control, simplicity, and transparency. These principles make it ideal for systems programming, where understanding and controlling every aspect of your code is critical. Zig avoids unnecessary abstractions and provides developers with direct access to memory, explicit error handling, and robust compile-time features. Unlike many modern languages that prioritize ease of use at the expense of performance or precision, Zig strikes a careful balance, giving you both power and clarity.

Zig also stands apart by rejecting some of the complexities and legacy baggage found in older languages like C. While it provides similar levels of low-level control, it eliminates common sources of frustration, such as undefined behavior or fragile macros. Zig's tooling and language features are designed to help developers write safer and more predictable code without sacrificing performance.

Setting Up Your Development Environment

The first step in learning Zig is to set up your development environment. Zig provides a simple, self-contained compiler that includes all the tools you need to write, build, and test your applications. This streamlined approach eliminates the need for additional dependencies, ensuring that you can get started quickly and focus on writing code.

To begin, download the latest version of Zig from the official website. The Zig compiler is available for a variety of platforms, including Windows, macOS, and Linux, and installation instructions are straightforward. Once installed, you can verify the setup by running the `zig version` command in your terminal or command prompt. This will confirm that the compiler is correctly installed and ready to use.

Writing Your First Zig Program

The best way to learn any programming language is by writing code, and Zig is no exception. A simple "Hello, World!" program is an excellent starting point, as it introduces the basics of Zig syntax and structure.

Here's what a "Hello, World!" program looks like in Zig:

```
const std = @import("std");


pub fn main() void {
    const stdout = std.io.getStdOut().writer();
```

```
        stdout.print("Hello,    World!\n",    .{})    catch
unreachable;

}
```

While this example might seem slightly verbose compared to other languages, every part of it serves a purpose. Zig avoids magical shortcuts, ensuring that you understand what your code does. The `@import("std")` statement imports Zig's standard library, while the `main` function is the program's entry point. By explicitly working with standard output and handling potential errors, Zig reinforces its philosophy of precision and predictability.

As you explore Zig further, you'll find that even this simple program showcases many of the language's strengths, such as its focus on clarity and explicit error handling.

Understanding Zig's Core Philosophy

Zig's design philosophy is one of its defining characteristics. Unlike many modern languages that prioritize developer convenience, Zig places a strong emphasis on giving you full control over your code. This makes it particularly well-suited for systems programming tasks, where performance, reliability, and correctness are paramount.

One of the most important aspects of Zig's philosophy is its explicitness. Zig encourages you to write code that is clear about its intentions, avoiding hidden behavior or implicit assumptions. For example, Zig requires you to handle all errors explicitly, rather than relying on exceptions or automatic error propagation. This approach ensures that your code is robust and predictable, even in complex scenarios.

Zig also provides powerful compile-time capabilities, allowing you to perform calculations, enforce constraints, and generate code at compile time. These features make it possible to write highly efficient and flexible programs without sacrificing readability or maintainability.

Features of Zig

Zig includes a range of features that set it apart from other programming languages. Some of the most notable include:

- **Manual Memory Management**: Zig gives you full control over memory allocation and deallocation, without the overhead of a garbage collector. This makes it ideal for applications where performance and resource usage are critical.
- **Error Handling**: Instead of exceptions, Zig uses a lightweight error-handling mechanism based on return values. This approach minimizes overhead and ensures that errors are always explicitly handled.
- **No Hidden Control Flow**: Zig avoids features like implicit type casting or automatic resource management that can introduce bugs or unexpected behavior.
- **Comptime**: Zig's compile-time execution allows you to perform calculations, generate code, and enforce constraints during compilation. This feature enables powerful optimizations and eliminates the need for complex runtime logic.
- **Cross-Compilation**: Zig includes a built-in cross-compilation toolchain, making it easy to build applications for multiple platforms from a single development environment.

These features make Zig a highly versatile language that can handle a wide range of programming tasks, from low-level systems development to high-performance applications.

Exploring Zig's Ecosystem

In addition to the language itself, Zig provides a rich ecosystem of tools and libraries that support a wide variety of use cases. The Zig standard library includes a comprehensive set of modules for tasks such as file I/O, networking, and concurrency. These modules are designed to be lightweight, efficient, and easy to use, reflecting Zig's overall philosophy.

Zig also integrates seamlessly with existing C codebases. The Zig compiler can directly import and call C functions, making it easy to incorporate Zig into existing projects or leverage existing libraries. This interoperability makes Zig a practical choice for developers who want to modernize their applications incrementally.

A Preview of What's Ahead

As you progress through Part 1, you'll gain a deeper understanding of Zig's syntax, tools, and capabilities. You'll learn how to write efficient and maintainable code, work with Zig's standard library, and harness its compile-time features to build powerful applications. By the end of this section, you'll have a solid foundation in Zig and be ready to explore more advanced topics in later parts of the book.

Zig's unique combination of simplicity, control, and modern features makes it an exciting language to learn and use. Whether you're developing embedded systems, writing performance-critical applications, or simply exploring a new programming paradigm, Zig offers a fresh perspective on what systems programming can be.

1.SETTING UP YOUR DEVELOPMENT ENVIRONMENT

Before you can dive into writing code with Zig, it's essential to properly set up your development environment. This process involves installing the Zig compiler, configuring your system, and familiarizing yourself with tools and IDEs that streamline the development process. Zig's design philosophy extends to its tooling, emphasizing simplicity and efficiency. As a result, getting started with Zig is straightforward, but setting up your environment correctly can significantly enhance your productivity and development experience.

INSTALLING ZIG

The Zig compiler is the heart of the development process, providing all the tools needed to build, test, and debug Zig programs. Unlike some programming languages that rely on a complex ecosystem of tools and dependencies, Zig is self-contained, making installation quick and painless.

To begin, visit the official Zig website and navigate to the downloads page. Zig provides precompiled binaries for major platforms, including Windows, macOS, and Linux. Select the appropriate version for your operating system and download the archive or installer.

For Windows users, download the `.zip` file, extract it to a directory of your choice, and add the extracted folder to your system's PATH environment variable. This allows you to run Zig commands from any terminal. On macOS, the simplest way to install Zig is via Homebrew. Run `brew install zig` in your terminal to download and install the latest version. Linux users can choose between downloading a binary archive or using a package manager, such as `apt` on Debian-based systems or `dnf` on Fedora.

After installation, verify that Zig is correctly installed by opening your terminal and running the following command:

zig version

If installed correctly, this will display the version of the Zig compiler. With Zig set up, you're ready to begin writing and running Zig programs.

IDEs, TOOLS, AND CONFIGURATION

While Zig does not impose any specific development environment, choosing the right IDE or editor can greatly improve your workflow. Zig is compatible with a wide range of tools, and its ecosystem includes plugins and extensions for popular text editors and IDEs. This flexibility allows you to tailor your environment to your preferences while taking full advantage of Zig's features.

Text Editors and IDEs

If you're new to Zig, a lightweight text editor is often the best place to start. Editors like Visual Studio Code, Sublime Text, and Vim offer powerful features with minimal configuration. However, for a more robust experience, full-featured IDEs like CLion can provide advanced capabilities like debugging, project management, and code analysis.

Visual Studio Code (VS Code):
 VS Code is one of the most popular editors for Zig due to its extensive ecosystem of extensions. To get started, install VS Code and add the Zig Language Support extension, which provides syntax highlighting, auto-completion, and error detection. You can further enhance your

experience with extensions for linting, debugging, and build system integration.

Sublime Text:
Sublime Text is a lightweight and responsive editor that supports Zig through community plugins. Install the "Zig Language" package via Package Control to enable syntax highlighting and basic language support.

Vim and Neovim:
For developers who prefer modal editing, Vim and Neovim offer highly customizable environments with Zig support. Install the Zig.vim plugin to enable syntax highlighting and formatting. Neovim users can additionally integrate the Language Server Protocol (LSP) for features like auto-completion and error detection.

CLion:
JetBrains' CLion is a powerful IDE designed for C and C++ development but also supports Zig through its CMake integration. This IDE is an excellent choice if you work on large projects or need advanced debugging and project management tools.

Configuring the Zig Language Server

The Zig Language Server (ZLS) is a tool that provides advanced features like auto-completion, code navigation, and on-the-fly error detection. ZLS integrates seamlessly with editors and IDEs that support the Language Server Protocol, such as VS Code, Vim, and Emacs.

To install ZLS, clone its repository from GitHub and build it using Zig itself:

```
git clone https://github.com/zigtools/zls.git

cd zls
```

```
zig build -Drelease-safe
```

Once installed, configure your editor to use ZLS as its language server. In VS Code, for example, you can add ZLS to your settings.json file or install the Zig Language Server extension for automatic configuration. With ZLS enabled, you'll gain access to powerful productivity features that make writing Zig code smoother and more efficient.

Build Tools and Debugging

While the Zig compiler includes a built-in build system, you may want to integrate other tools to enhance your workflow. Zig's build system uses a declarative syntax, making it easy to define build steps, manage dependencies, and configure compiler options. Unlike other build tools like Make or Ninja, Zig's build system is tightly integrated with the language, offering a more seamless experience.

For debugging, Zig supports integration with GDB and LLDB, the widely-used debugging tools for C and C++ development. Most modern IDEs, such as VS Code and CLion, include built-in debugging interfaces that work with these tools. Simply configure your debugger to recognize Zig executables, and you'll be able to set breakpoints, inspect variables, and step through your code with ease.

Version Management

If you're working on multiple projects or contributing to the Zig compiler itself, you may need to manage different versions of Zig on your system. Tools like zigup simplify this process by allowing you to install and switch between multiple versions of Zig. This is particularly useful if you want to experiment with Zig's nightly builds, which often include cutting-edge features and improvements.

To install `zigup`, follow the instructions in its GitHub repository. Once installed, you can use commands like `zigup install` and `zigup switch` to manage your Zig installations. This flexibility ensures that you can always use the version of Zig best suited to your needs.

Customizing Your Workflow

Beyond the basic setup, you can further customize your development environment to align with your workflow. For example, if you frequently write tests, consider configuring your editor to run Zig's built-in test runner automatically. Similarly, if you work on large codebases, enable features like linting and static analysis to catch errors early.

Some developers also use containerized environments, such as Docker, to ensure consistent builds across different machines. By creating a Dockerfile that includes the Zig compiler and any necessary dependencies, you can standardize your development setup and eliminate potential compatibility issues.

Setting up your Zig development environment is a straightforward process that involves installing the compiler, selecting an editor or IDE, and configuring tools like ZLS and debugging interfaces. While Zig's simplicity means you can get started with minimal effort, taking the time to customize your environment can greatly enhance your productivity and enjoyment of the language. Whether you're a beginner exploring Zig for the first time or an experienced developer diving into systems programming, a well-configured environment lays the foundation for success.

3.ZIG BASICS

To write efficient, reliable, and maintainable code in Zig, it's crucial to understand its fundamental building blocks. This chapter introduces the basics of Zig, including its syntax, variables, data types, functions, control flow, error handling, and testing. Together, these concepts form the core of Zig programming, giving you the tools to write your first programs and build a solid foundation for more advanced topics.

SYNTAX, VARIABLES, AND DATA TYPES

Zig's syntax is designed to be clean, minimal, and free of ambiguity. It borrows ideas from C while introducing modern enhancements that improve readability and safety. This section provides a detailed look at how to declare and work with variables and data types in Zig.

Basic Syntax

Zig's code structure is straightforward, with a consistent style that avoids unnecessary complexity. A typical Zig program starts with the const keyword to import the standard library:

```
const std = @import("std");
```

The entry point of a Zig program is the main function, defined as:

```
pub fn main() void {

    // Program logic goes here

}
```

Functions are marked `pub` to indicate they are publicly accessible, and the return type follows the function declaration (`void` in this case). Zig requires explicit type annotations or inferences for variables, ensuring that all data types are well-defined.

Variables

Variables in Zig are declared using the `var` keyword for mutable variables and the `const` keyword for immutable ones. For example:

var count: i32 = 10; // Mutable variable

const pi: f64 = 3.14159; // Immutable variable

Zig encourages the use of `const` whenever possible to promote immutability, a practice that improves code clarity and prevents unintended side effects.

Zig also supports type inference for variables. If you initialize a variable with a value, the compiler can deduce its type:

const greeting = "Hello, Zig!"; // Type inferred as []const u8 (a string)

Data Types

Zig's type system includes a wide range of primitive types, such as integers, floating-point numbers, booleans, and pointers. The most common types are:

- **Integers:** Zig supports signed (i8, i16, i32, i64) and unsigned (u8, u16, u32, u64) integers.

- **Floating-Point Numbers:** Use $f16$, $f32$, or $f64$ for half-precision, single-precision, and double-precision floating-point values, respectively.
- **Booleans:** Represented by the bool type, which can be either true or false.
- **Strings:** Strings in Zig are arrays of UTF-8 bytes ([]const u8). They are immutable by default.

Zig also includes advanced types, such as arrays, slices, structs, enums, and unions, which you'll explore as you progress.

FUNCTIONS AND CONTROL FLOW

Functions and control flow structures are essential tools for organizing and executing logic in your programs. Zig's approach to these concepts is straightforward yet powerful, offering precise control over execution.

Functions

Functions in Zig are defined using the fn keyword, followed by the function name, parameters, and return type. For example:

```
fn add(a: i32, b: i32) i32 {
    return a + b;
}
```

Here, the add function takes two i32 parameters and returns an i32. Zig requires you to explicitly specify the return type, reinforcing its philosophy of clarity and explicitness. If a function does not return a value, use void as the return type.

Zig also supports anonymous functions, function pointers, and first-class functions, making it a flexible choice for functional programming patterns.

Control Flow

Zig provides standard control flow constructs, including `if`, `else`, `while`, `for`, and `switch`. These constructs are designed to be explicit and predictable, avoiding surprises commonly found in other languages.

Conditional Statements

Conditional logic in Zig is straightforward:

```
if (count > 10) {
    std.debug.print("Count is greater than 10\n", .{});
} else {
    std.debug.print("Count is 10 or less\n", .{});
}
```

Zig requires parentheses around the condition but uses braces to delimit the code block. Unlike some languages, there are no implicit conversions between types, so conditions must evaluate to a boolean.

Loops

Zig supports both `while` and `for` loops for iteration. A `while` loop continues as long as its condition evaluates to `true`:

```
var i: i32 = 0;
while (i < 5) : (i += 1) {
```

```
    std.debug.print("i = {}\n", .{i});
}
```

The optional `: (i += 1)` syntax executes after each iteration, simplifying common patterns.

The `for` loop iterates over arrays, slices, or ranges:

```
const arr = [_]i32{1, 2, 3, 4, 5};
for (arr) |item| {
    std.debug.print("Item: {}\n", .{item});
}
```

Here, `|item|` represents the loop variable for each element in the array.

Switch Statements

The `switch` statement handles multiple conditions cleanly:

```
const color = "red";
switch (color) {
    "red" => std.debug.print("Color is red\n", .{}),
    "blue" => std.debug.print("Color is blue\n", .{}),
    else => std.debug.print("Unknown color\n", .{}),
}
```

The `else` branch is required unless all cases are covered, ensuring exhaustive matching.

ERROR HANDLING

Error handling in Zig is a key aspect of its philosophy. Instead of exceptions or implicit error propagation, Zig uses an explicit error system based on return values. This approach is safer and more predictable, as every error must be explicitly handled.

Declaring and Returning Errors

Errors in Zig are declared using the ! symbol before the return type:

```
fn divide(a: i32, b: i32) !i32 {

    if (b == 0) {

        return error.DivideByZero;

    }

    return a / b;

}
```

Here, the function `divide` returns either an `i32` or an error. Errors are declared using the `error.` namespace.

Error Propagation

Zig provides the `try` keyword to propagate errors. If an error occurs, it is passed up the call stack:

const result = try divide(10, 2);

std.debug.print("Result: {}\n", .{result});

The `try` keyword ensures that errors are handled explicitly, improving code safety and readability.

Catching Errors

To handle errors directly, use the `catch` keyword:

```
const result = divide(10, 0) catch |err| {
    std.debug.print("Error: {}\n", .{err});
    return;
};
```

The `catch` block executes if an error occurs, allowing you to respond accordingly.

Testing Basics

Zig includes a built-in testing framework that makes it easy to write and run tests. Testing is a first-class citizen in Zig, encouraging developers to adopt a test-driven approach.

Writing Tests

Tests in Zig are defined using the `test` keyword, followed by a descriptive name:

```
test "addition works" {
    const result = add(2, 3);
    std.testing.expect(result == 5);
}
```

The `std.testing.expect` function asserts that a condition is true. If the condition fails, the test reports an error.

Running Tests

To run tests, use the `zig test` command:

```
zig test your_file.zig
```

This compiles and executes all tests in the specified file, displaying the results in the terminal.

Advanced Testing Features

Zig's testing framework supports more advanced features, such as mocking, benchmarking, and test isolation. These capabilities allow you to thoroughly validate your code, ensuring that it behaves as expected under a variety of conditions.

Understanding Zig's syntax, variables, data types, functions, control flow, error handling, and testing basics is essential for becoming proficient in the language. These foundational concepts equip you with the tools to write efficient, reliable, and maintainable code. As you continue to explore Zig, these basics will serve as the building blocks for more advanced features and patterns, enabling you to unlock the full potential of this powerful programming language.

Part 2:

CORE CONCEPTS AND LANGUAGE FEATURES

Part 2 of this book dives deeper into Zig's core concepts and language features, building on the foundational knowledge introduced earlier. While Part 1 provided a basic understanding of syntax, variables, and functions, this section explores the intricacies that make Zig a powerful tool for systems programming. It's here that the language's true potential comes to light, showcasing its capabilities for writing efficient, portable, and maintainable code.

Zig is more than a language for solving programming problems; it's a philosophy of explicitness, control, and simplicity. These qualities are reflected in its design and features, which emphasize developer intention while minimizing overhead and ambiguity. Whether you're working on embedded systems, game engines, or cross-platform applications, understanding Zig's core concepts is critical to unlocking its full potential.

The Philosophy of Zig

Zig stands out in the programming world because of its adherence to a design philosophy that prioritizes clarity and explicit behavior. This philosophy permeates every aspect of the language, from how it handles memory and concurrency to its robust error management model. Zig's core concepts revolve around providing developers with complete control over their programs, a trait that is often missing in higher-level languages.

One of Zig's defining features is its lack of hidden behaviors. Unlike many modern programming languages, Zig avoids implicit allocations, garbage collection, or runtime surprises. Instead, developers are encouraged to be explicit about how resources are managed, how errors are handled, and how data flows through their programs. This approach not only results in faster and more predictable code but also encourages a deeper understanding of the underlying systems.

A Strong Foundation in Systems Programming

As a systems programming language, Zig provides direct access to low-level operations without sacrificing developer productivity. This balance makes it particularly appealing to those who need fine-grained control over performance and resources. Whether you are allocating memory, working with raw pointers, or interfacing with hardware, Zig's feature set ensures that you can operate with precision.

Zig's approach to memory management, for example, reflects its emphasis on control and safety. Instead of relying on automatic garbage collection, Zig provides tools for manual memory management, empowering developers to make decisions based on the specific needs of their applications. Combined with features like optional runtime checks and compile-time analysis, Zig ensures that developers can write code that is both efficient and reliable.

Portable and Cross-Platform Development

Another core strength of Zig lies in its focus on portability. Writing software that runs seamlessly across multiple platforms can be a daunting challenge, but Zig simplifies this process with its built-in cross-compilation capabilities. The Zig compiler can target various platforms and architectures without requiring additional tools or configurations, making it an ideal choice for developers working in heterogeneous environments.

Additionally, Zig's standard library is designed with portability in mind. It abstracts away platform-specific details while maintaining transparency and control. This allows developers to write code that is both portable and tailored to the nuances of each target environment. These capabilities make Zig a compelling choice for projects that demand consistent behavior across diverse platforms, such as embedded systems, games, and cloud applications.

Part 2 of this book also introduces Zig's advanced language features, which set it apart from other systems programming languages. Features like comptime (compile-time execution) allow developers to execute code during compilation, enabling powerful metaprogramming capabilities. With comptime, you can generate efficient, specialized code, validate input, or even replace runtime operations with compile-time logic. This unique feature simplifies the development of complex systems, reducing both runtime overhead and potential sources of bugs.

Zig's error-handling model is another standout feature explored in this section. Unlike exceptions in other languages, Zig uses an explicit error return mechanism, which promotes clarity and forces developers to confront potential errors head-on. Combined with features like error unions and error propagation, this model ensures that error handling is both robust and predictable. Other topics in this part of the book include working with structs, enums, and unions, as well as leveraging Zig's support for generics and type safety. These features make it easier to write reusable, type-safe code without introducing the complexity often associated with template-based systems in languages like C++.

Part 2 is where Zig truly begins to reveal its inner workings. Through these chapters, you'll gain a deeper appreciation for the language's design principles and learn how to harness its features effectively. The goal is not only to teach you how Zig works but also to help you think like a Zig programmer—writing code that is deliberate, efficient, and well-structured.

This part of the book also delves into Zig's approach to concurrency, testing, and debugging, ensuring you are equipped to handle real-world challenges. By the end of Part 2, you'll have a comprehensive understanding of Zig's capabilities and be prepared to build software that is both performant and maintainable.

While Part 1 introduced you to the basics, Part 2 equips you with the tools and knowledge needed to tackle complex programming challenges. As you explore these core concepts and features, you'll discover why Zig has become a favorite among systems programmers and those who value performance and control. This journey will deepen your understanding of the language and prepare you for the more advanced topics covered later in the book.

1.MEMORY MANAGEMENT IN ZIG

Memory management is one of the most critical aspects of systems programming, and Zig excels in offering precise control over memory without sacrificing safety or readability. Unlike languages with garbage collection or automatic memory handling, Zig places the responsibility of managing memory directly in the hands of developers. This explicit control ensures that Zig programs are efficient and predictable, qualities essential for performance-critical applications like operating systems, game engines, and embedded systems.

Zig's memory management model is centered around manual principles, with a robust system of allocators and deallocators to handle dynamic memory. By adhering to these principles, developers can manage memory more effectively while avoiding common pitfalls like memory leaks, dangling pointers, and undefined behavior. This section explores Zig's memory management principles and its allocator system, providing a comprehensive understanding of how to work with memory in Zig.

MANUAL MEMORY MANAGEMENT PRINCIPLES

Zig's philosophy of explicitness extends to memory management, requiring developers to take full control of resource allocation and deallocation. Unlike higher-level languages that abstract memory handling, Zig's approach offers unparalleled control over how memory is allocated, accessed, and freed. This explicitness reduces runtime surprises and makes the memory lifecycle more predictable.

Explicit Allocation and Deallocation

In Zig, memory is not automatically allocated or garbage-collected. Instead, developers must explicitly request and release memory using allocators. For instance, when creating a dynamic array, you must allocate memory for the array and later deallocate it once it is no longer needed:

```
const std = @import("std");


pub fn main() !void {

    const allocator = std.heap.page_allocator;


    // Allocate memory for an array of 10 integers

    const array = try allocator.alloc(i32, 10);


    // Use the array for some operations

    array[0] = 42;


    // Free the memory when done

    allocator.free(array);

}
```

This code demonstrates two key principles of Zig's memory management: memory is allocated through an allocator, and the programmer is responsible for freeing it. This explicitness eliminates ambiguity, ensuring that memory usage is transparent and deliberate.

Resource Ownership and Lifetime

Zig emphasizes the importance of resource ownership and lifetime. When you allocate memory, you are considered the owner of that memory, and it is your responsibility to manage its lifetime. This ownership model aligns with Zig's error handling and safety guarantees, ensuring that memory is neither freed prematurely nor left dangling.

For example, when passing a dynamically allocated resource to a function, it is essential to clearly define whether the function assumes ownership of that resource. If the function takes ownership, it should deallocate the memory; otherwise, the caller remains responsible.

Avoiding Undefined Behavior

Undefined behavior (UB) is one of the most significant challenges in manual memory management. Issues like accessing freed memory, writing outside allocated bounds, or leaking memory can lead to serious bugs. Zig mitigates these risks by offering runtime safety checks (enabled in debug builds) and compile-time analysis tools. These features help identify potential issues before they manifest in production, striking a balance between control and safety.

ALLOCATORS AND DEALLOCATORS

Allocators are a core feature of Zig's memory management model. They provide a unified interface for allocating, resizing, and freeing memory, making it easier to manage resources across diverse use cases. Zig's standard library includes a variety of allocators, each optimized for different scenarios, from high-performance heap allocators to stack-based temporary allocators.

What is an Allocator?

An allocator in Zig is an abstraction that defines how memory is allocated and managed. Allocators follow a common interface, consisting of three primary operations: `alloc`, `realloc`, and `free`. These operations are used to allocate new memory, resize existing memory, and release memory, respectively.

For example, the `std.heap.page_allocator` is a general-purpose allocator provided by Zig:

```zig
const std = @import("std");


pub fn main() !void {
    const allocator = std.heap.page_allocator;


    const buffer = try allocator.alloc(u8, 100); // Allocate 100 bytes
                    const resized_buffer = try allocator.realloc(buffer, 150); // Resize to 150 bytes


    allocator.free(resized_buffer); // Free the memory

}
```

In this example, the `alloc` function allocates a block of memory, `realloc` adjusts its size, and `free` releases the memory when it is no longer needed.

Types of Allocators

Zig provides several types of allocators, each suited to specific use cases. Understanding these allocators is key to selecting the right tool for your application.

1. **Heap Allocators**
   Heap allocators, like `std.heap.page_allocator`, are the most versatile and commonly used allocators in Zig. They allocate memory from the heap, making them suitable for dynamic and long-lived data structures. However, heap allocations can be relatively slow and require explicit deallocation.

2. **Stack Allocators**
   Stack allocators, such as `std.heap.FixedBufferAllocator`, allocate memory from a fixed-size buffer. These are ideal for temporary or short-lived allocations, as they operate quickly and require minimal overhead. However, they are limited by the size of the buffer and should not be used for data with unpredictable lifetimes.

3. **Arena Allocators**
   Arena allocators allow you to allocate multiple blocks of memory in a single operation and release them all at once. This approach is efficient for batch allocations and deallocations, as it reduces fragmentation and simplifies resource management. The `std.heap.ArenaAllocator` is a popular choice for this pattern.

4. **Custom Allocators**

   Zig allows you to implement your own allocators by adhering to the allocator interface. Custom allocators are useful for specialized scenarios where standard allocators are not optimal.

Using Allocators in Functions

When writing functions that allocate memory, it is a common practice to pass an allocator as an argument. This approach makes the function more flexible and reusable, as it can work with any allocator:

```zig
fn createBuffer(allocator: *std.mem.Allocator, size: usize) ![]u8 {

    return try allocator.alloc(u8, size);

}


pub fn main() !void {

    const allocator = std.heap.page_allocator;

    const buffer = try createBuffer(&allocator, 256);


    // Use the buffer

    buffer[0] = 42;


    allocator.free(buffer);
```

```
}
```

By passing the allocator explicitly, you give the caller control over how memory is managed, aligning with Zig's emphasis on explicitness and flexibility.

Deallocating Memory

Proper deallocation is critical to preventing memory leaks. In Zig, every allocation must be paired with a corresponding deallocation. Failing to free memory can lead to resource exhaustion, especially in long-running applications. Zig provides tools like defer to simplify cleanup:

```
pub fn main() !void {

    const allocator = std.heap.page_allocator;

    const array = try allocator.alloc(i32, 5);

    defer allocator.free(array); // Automatically frees
memory at the end of the scope


    // Use the array

    array[0] = 10;

}
```

The defer statement ensures that allocator.free is called automatically when the scope exits, reducing the risk of forgetting to free memory manually.

Allocator Safety and Debugging

Debugging memory issues can be challenging, but Zig provides features to make this process easier. For example, Zig's standard library includes `std.heap.DebugAllocator`, which wraps an existing allocator and tracks memory allocations, helping you detect leaks, double frees, and other issues during development.

```
const std = @import("std");


pub fn main() !void {
                        var     debug_allocator     =
std.heap.DebugAllocator.init(std.heap.page_allocator);

    const allocator = &debug_allocator.allocator;


    const buffer = try allocator.alloc(u8, 100);

    allocator.free(buffer);


    // Check for memory leaks

    try debug_allocator.report();

}
```

The `DebugAllocator` reports any mismatches between allocations and deallocations, providing valuable insights into memory usage and helping you identify potential problems early.

Zig's approach to memory management is rooted in manual principles that prioritize control, safety, and transparency. By explicitly allocating and deallocating memory, developers can write efficient and predictable programs without relying on garbage collection or automatic abstractions. Zig's allocator system further enhances this process, offering flexible tools for managing memory across diverse scenarios.

Understanding these principles and tools is essential for mastering Zig's memory management model. By adhering to best practices, using the right allocators for each context, and leveraging debugging tools, you can manage memory effectively and avoid common pitfalls. With these skills, you'll be well-equipped to build robust and performant applications in Zig, harnessing the full power of its low-level capabilities.

5. ERROR HANDLING AND SAFETY IN ZIG

Error handling is a critical aspect of any programming language, and Zig takes a unique approach that prioritizes simplicity, explicitness, and safety. Unlike languages that rely on exceptions or extensive runtime error handling, Zig employs a model centered around error unions and propagation. This model ensures that error handling is predictable, concise, and integrated into the language's core design.

In Zig, errors are not unexpected events that disrupt the flow of a program. Instead, they are first-class citizens that are treated as a natural part of the program's logic. By making errors explicit and requiring developers to address them directly, Zig eliminates ambiguity and reduces the likelihood of bugs caused by unhandled or unexpected failures.

This section delves into Zig's approach to error handling, exploring how error unions and catch patterns work, and how they contribute to the language's commitment to safety and robustness.

ZIG'S APPROACH TO ERRORS

Zig's error-handling model is designed to be both simple and expressive, enabling developers to write reliable code without the overhead of exceptions or complex error hierarchies. The core principles of Zig's error-handling philosophy include explicitness, control, and composability.

Errors as Values

In Zig, errors are not exceptions that propagate through an implicit mechanism. Instead, they are values that are explicitly represented in the type system. This approach makes error handling a visible part of the program's structure, encouraging developers to think carefully about how errors are managed and propagated.

Errors in Zig are declared using the `error` keyword, and they are typically defined as part of a function's return type. For example:

```
const std = @import("std");


fn divide(a: i32, b: i32) !i32 {

    if (b == 0) {

        return error.DivideByZero;

    }

    return a / b;

}
```

In this example, the `divide` function explicitly declares that it may return an error of type `error.DivideByZero` if an invalid operation is attempted. Errors are part of the function's return type, making them explicit and predictable.

Error Propagation

Zig simplifies error propagation with the `try` keyword. The `try` keyword is used to call a function that can return an error. If the function succeeds, its value is returned; if it fails, the error is propagated up the call stack. For example:

```
fn calculateResult() !void {
```

```
    const result = try divide(10, 0);

    std.debug.print("Result: {}\n", .{result});

}
```

If `divide` returns an error, the `try` statement automatically propagates it, ensuring that the calling function handles the error appropriately. This approach reduces boilerplate code while keeping error handling explicit.

Returning Errors Explicitly

In addition to using `try`, developers can also explicitly check and handle errors returned by functions. For example:

```
fn calculate() void {

    const result = divide(10, 0);

    switch (result) {

        error.DivideByZero => std.debug.print("Error:
Division by zero\n", .{}),

            else => std.debug.print("Result: {}\n",
.{result}),

    }

}
```

This pattern allows developers to handle specific errors directly, providing flexibility and control over error management.

Error Unions

Error unions are a fundamental feature of Zig's error-handling model. An error union is a type that represents either a successful value or an error. For instance, the return type `!i32` indicates that a function can return either an `i32` or an error.

Defining and Using Error Unions

Error unions are used extensively in Zig to make error handling a first-class concern. Consider the following example:

```
fn safeDivide(a: i32, b: i32) !i32 {

    if (b == 0) {

        return error.DivideByZero;

    }

    return a / b;

}
```

Here, the `safeDivide` function returns an error union `!i32`, meaning it can either return an integer or an error. This type is explicit and self-documenting, ensuring that developers are aware of the function's behavior.

Matching Error Unions

Zig provides tools to work with error unions efficiently. The `catch` keyword allows developers to handle errors inline:

```
pub fn main() void {

    const result = safeDivide(10, 0) catch |err| {
```

```
    std.debug.print("Caught error: {}\n", .{err});

    return;

};

std.debug.print("Result: {}\n", .{result});

}
```

In this example, the `catch` block intercepts any errors returned by `safeDivide` and handles them accordingly. This approach keeps error-handling logic close to the source of the error, improving code readability.

Default Values with Catch

The `catch` keyword can also be used to provide a default value in case of an error:

```
pub fn main() void {

    const result = safeDivide(10, 0) catch 0; //
Default to 0 if an error occurs

    std.debug.print("Result: {}\n", .{result});

}
```

This pattern is particularly useful for cases where a fallback value is appropriate and simplifies the handling of non-critical errors.

Patterns for Error Handling

Zig's error-handling model supports various patterns that allow developers to manage errors effectively. These patterns range from simple propagation to detailed error recovery and logging.

Propagating Errors

Error propagation is the most common pattern in Zig. By using the `try` keyword, developers can pass errors up the call stack until they are handled by a higher-level function. This approach is efficient for situations where a function cannot recover from an error on its own.

```
pub fn main() !void {

    const result = try safeDivide(10, 0);

    std.debug.print("Result: {}\n", .{result});

}
```

Handling Specific Errors

In some cases, you may want to handle specific errors differently. Zig's `switch` statement is ideal for this purpose:

```
fn handleErrorExample() void {

    const result = safeDivide(10, 0);

    switch (result) {

        error.DivideByZero => std.debug.print("Cannot divide by zero\n", .{}),

        else => std.debug.print("Success: {}\n", .{result}),
```

```
    }
}
```

By matching specific errors, you can implement customized error-handling logic while maintaining clarity and precision.

Logging and Debugging

For debugging purposes, Zig's standard library provides tools like `std.debug.print` to log error messages and additional information. This is especially useful when tracking down issues in complex programs.

```
pub fn main() void {

    const result = safeDivide(10, 0);

    if (result) |value| {

        std.debug.print("Result: {}\n", .{value});

    } else |err| {

            std.debug.print("Error encountered: {}\n",
.{err});

    }

}
```

Safety Through Explicitness

Zig's error-handling model is designed to reduce the risk of unhandled errors and undefined behavior. By making errors explicit and integrating them into the type system, Zig ensures that developers cannot ignore potential failures. This model, combined with compile-time checks and optional runtime safety checks, makes Zig a robust and reliable choice for building systems that demand high levels of correctness.

By treating errors as values, leveraging error unions, and adopting clear propagation and handling patterns, Zig promotes a disciplined approach to error management that is both practical and intuitive. This explicitness enhances safety, predictability, and developer confidence, ensuring that Zig applications can handle errors gracefully without sacrificing performance or control.

6. CONCURRENCY AND ASYNCHRONOUS PROGRAMMING IN ZIG

Concurrency and asynchronous programming are fundamental to creating high-performance, responsive, and scalable software systems. Zig's approach to these concepts reflects its philosophy of explicitness, simplicity, and efficiency. By providing native support for asynchronous programming through `async` and `await`, along with the tools to build lightweight concurrency models, Zig enables developers to write concurrent code without relying on heavy abstractions or third-party libraries.

This section explores Zig's approach to concurrency and asynchronous programming, detailing the use of `async` and `await`, and how to construct lightweight concurrency models that balance performance with clarity.

Zig's Approach to Concurrency

Concurrency in Zig is grounded in a cooperative model where tasks yield control voluntarily to facilitate efficient multitasking. Unlike preemptive multitasking systems that depend on operating system threads, Zig's concurrency model is designed to minimize overhead and maximize control. This approach aligns with the language's goals of providing low-level control while maintaining safety and performance.

By using async/await syntax and custom concurrency patterns, developers can design programs that perform multiple tasks concurrently, making optimal use of system resources. Zig does not impose a specific runtime, allowing developers to integrate its concurrency model into a wide range of environments, from embedded systems to high-performance servers.

USING ASYNC AND AWAIT

The `async` and `await` keywords are central to Zig's asynchronous programming model. They enable the creation of non-blocking tasks that can pause execution and resume later, allowing other tasks to execute in the meantime. This model is ideal for I/O-bound operations, network communication, and other scenarios where waiting for external resources would otherwise block the program.

Writing Asynchronous Functions

An asynchronous function in Zig is defined using the `async` keyword. This indicates that the function may pause and yield control at certain points during its execution. For example:

```
const std = @import("std");
```

```
pub async fn fetchData(url: []const u8) ![]u8 {
    // Simulate a network request
    const data = try std.net.tcpConnect(url);
    return data.readAll() catch error.NetworkIssue;
}
```

In this example, `fetchData` is an asynchronous function that simulates fetching data from a network. The `async` keyword allows the function to yield control while waiting for the network operation to complete.

Calling Asynchronous Functions with `await`

To call an asynchronous function, you use the `await` keyword. This pauses the current function's execution until the asynchronous task completes and returns its result. For example:

```
pub fn main() !void {

                        const       data      =       await
fetchData("https://example.com");

    std.debug.print("Fetched data: {}\n", .{data});

}
```

The `await` keyword ensures that the program does not block while waiting for the asynchronous task, allowing other tasks to execute concurrently.

Combining Multiple Asynchronous Tasks

Zig's concurrency model makes it easy to work with multiple asynchronous tasks simultaneously. For example, you can launch several asynchronous functions and wait for all of them to complete:

```
pub async fn main() !void {

    const task1 = fetchData("https://example1.com");

    const task2 = fetchData("https://example2.com");

    const task3 = fetchData("https://example3.com");


    const result1 = await task1;
```

```
    const result2 = await task2;

    const result3 = await task3;


    std.debug.print("Results: {}, {}, {}\n", .{result1,
result2, result3});

}
```

This approach enables concurrent execution of tasks, significantly improving performance in scenarios where tasks are independent and can run in parallel.

BUILDING LIGHTWEIGHT CONCURRENCY MODELS

Zig's design encourages the development of lightweight concurrency models that do not rely on threads or heavyweight constructs. Instead, Zig allows you to create task-based concurrency models tailored to your application's requirements.

Tasks and Executors

A common pattern in Zig is to create an executor that manages the scheduling and execution of asynchronous tasks. An executor is responsible for running tasks, managing their lifetimes, and coordinating their interactions. For example:

```
const std = @import("std");


pub fn main() !void {

    var executor = std.async.Executor.init();
```

```
    defer executor.deinit();


    try executor.run(fetchData("https://example.com"));
}
```

This example demonstrates a simple executor that runs a single asynchronous task. Executors can be extended to support more complex scenarios, such as scheduling multiple tasks, handling task priorities, or implementing timeouts.

Event-Driven Concurrency

Zig's concurrency model integrates well with event-driven programming, where tasks respond to events such as I/O completions, user input, or timers. For example, you can use Zig's standard library to create an event loop that processes asynchronous events:

```
pub async fn eventLoop() !void {

    while (true) {

        const event = await waitForEvent();

        handleEvent(event);

    }

}
```

In this model, the eventLoop function continuously waits for events and processes them as they arrive. This approach is efficient and scalable, as it avoids the overhead of creating and managing threads for each task.

Custom Schedulers

For advanced use cases, Zig allows you to implement custom schedulers that control how tasks are executed. A scheduler can determine the order in which tasks run, how resources are allocated, and how task lifetimes are managed. This level of control is particularly useful for real-time systems, embedded applications, or specialized high-performance environments.

Error Handling in Asynchronous Code

Error handling in Zig's asynchronous model follows the same principles as in synchronous code. Errors are explicitly represented in the type system and must be handled or propagated using `try` or `catch`.

Propagating Errors in Asynchronous Tasks

Errors in asynchronous functions can be propagated using the `try` keyword. For example:

```zig
pub async fn main() !void {

    const data = try fetchData("https://example.com");

    std.debug.print("Fetched data: {}\n", .{data});

}
```

If `fetchData` encounters an error, it is automatically propagated to the calling function, ensuring that errors are handled consistently.

Catching Errors in Asynchronous Code

To handle specific errors, you can use the `catch` keyword. This is particularly useful when you need to recover from an error or provide a fallback value:

```zig
pub async fn main() void {

const data = fetchData("https://example.com") catch |err| {

std.debug.print("Error fetching data: {}\n", .{err});

return;

};

std.debug.print("Fetched data: {}\n", .{data});

}
```

This pattern keeps error-handling logic close to the source of the error, improving readability and maintainability.

Performance and Safety

Zig's concurrency model is designed to be lightweight and efficient, minimizing the overhead associated with traditional threading models. By leveraging cooperative multitasking and explicit error handling, Zig ensures that concurrent code is not only performant but also safe and predictable.

Furthermore, Zig's compile-time checks and optional runtime safety features help catch common concurrency issues, such as race conditions or deadlocks, during development. These tools provide an additional layer of reliability without compromising the language's low-level capabilities.

Concurrency and asynchronous programming are essential for building modern, high-performance software, and Zig's approach provides a powerful yet simple model for achieving this. By combining native support for `async` and `await` with the ability to construct lightweight concurrency models, Zig offers developers the flexibility to create scalable and efficient programs tailored to their specific needs.

Through explicit task management, seamless error handling, and robust safety features, Zig empowers developers to write concurrent code that is both reliable and performant. Whether you're building networked services, event-driven systems, or real-time applications, Zig's concurrency model provides the tools you need to harness the full potential of asynchronous programming.

WORKING WITH TYPES IN ZIG

Zig's type system is designed to be both powerful and intuitive, offering developers the tools to write expressive and maintainable code while maintaining low-level control over memory and performance. Central to Zig's type system are constructs like structs, enums, and unions, which allow for the creation of complex, user-defined types. Zig also provides features like generics and type inference, enabling developers to write flexible and reusable code without unnecessary verbosity.

This section explores how to work with types in Zig, delving into the intricacies of structs, enums, and unions, and examining how generics and type inference can streamline the development process.

STRUCTS: ORGANIZING DATA

Structs in Zig are foundational for organizing related data into a single, coherent type. They allow developers to group multiple fields together, each with its own name and type, making code more structured and readable. Structs are used extensively in Zig for representing objects, managing state, and encapsulating data in a type-safe manner.

Defining Structs

To define a struct in Zig, use the `struct` keyword followed by a block of field definitions. For example:

```
const std = @import("std");


const Point = struct {
    x: i32,
```

```
    y: i32,

};


pub fn main() void {

    const p = Point{ .x = 10, .y = 20 };

    std.debug.print("Point: ({}, {})\n", .{p.x, p.y});

}
```

In this example, the `Point` struct groups two integer fields, `x` and `y`, representing a point in a two-dimensional space. You can access struct fields using the dot (`.`) operator.

Methods on Structs

Zig allows you to define methods on structs by declaring functions inside the struct block. These methods can operate on the struct's fields and provide functionality specific to the type:

```
const Point = struct {

    x: i32,

    y: i32,


    fn distance(self: Point) i32 {

        return self.x * self.x + self.y * self.y;

    }
```

```
};

pub fn main() void {

    const p = Point{ .x = 3, .y = 4 };

    std.debug.print("Distance: {}\n", .{p.distance()});

}
```

Methods make structs more versatile by embedding logic alongside data, fostering encapsulation and improving code organization.

Enums: Defining Named Values

Enums in Zig are a way to define a set of named, constant values that represent distinct options or states. They are often used for scenarios where a value can be one of a predefined set of possibilities, such as error codes, states, or modes.

Defining Enums

An enum is defined using the enum keyword, followed by a list of cases. Each case represents a distinct value:

```
const Direction = enum {

    North,

    South,

    East,

    West,
```

```
};

pub fn main() void {

    const dir = Direction.North;

    std.debug.print("Direction: {}\n", .{dir});

}
```

Enums provide strong type safety and improve code readability by replacing arbitrary constants with meaningful names.

Enum Values and Payloads

Enums can also associate values or payloads with their cases, making them more versatile for representing complex states:

```
const Command = enum {

    Move { x: i32, y: i32 },

    Stop,

};


pub fn main() void {

    const cmd = Command.Move{ .x = 10, .y = 20 };

    switch (cmd) {

        Command.Move => |move| std.debug.print("Move to
({}, {})\n", .{move.x, move.y}),
```

```
        Command.Stop => std.debug.print("Stop\n", .{}),

    }

}
```

In this example, the `Command` enum has a `Move` case that carries additional data, demonstrating how enums can encapsulate both value and context.

Unions: Flexible Data Representation

Unions in Zig are used for types where only one of several possible fields is active at a given time. They provide a way to conserve memory and define flexible data structures.

Defining Unions

A union is defined using the `union` keyword. Unlike structs, a union allocates memory for only one of its fields, based on what is currently active:

```
const Data = union {

    i: i32,

    f: f32,

};



pub fn main() void {
                \
    var d: Data = Data{i: 42};

    std.debug.print("Data as integer: {}\n", .{d.i});
```

```
}
```

Tagged Unions

Tagged unions combine the flexibility of unions with the safety of enums. They associate a tag with each field, ensuring that only the active field is accessed:

```
const Data = union(enum) {

    Int: i32,

    Float: f32,

};


pub fn main() void {

    const d = Data.Int(42);

    switch (d) {

        Data.Int => |value| std.debug.print("Integer:
{}\n", .{value}),

        Data.Float => |value| std.debug.print("Float:
{}\n", .{value}),

    }

}
```

Tagged unions reduce the risk of accessing the wrong field, making them ideal for scenarios where type safety is critical.

GENERICS: WRITING REUSABLE CODE

Generics in Zig enable the creation of flexible and reusable functions and types that work with a variety of data types. Generics are implemented using compile-time parameters, which allow code to adapt to different types during compilation.

Generic Functions

A generic function in Zig uses a parameterized type to accept inputs of varying types. For example:

```
fn add(T: type, a: T, b: T) T {

    return a + b;

}


pub fn main() void {

    const intResult = add(i32, 10, 20);

    const floatResult = add(f32, 1.5, 2.5);

        std.debug.print("Int:    {},    Float:    {}\n",
.{intResult, floatResult});

}
```

The add function works with any type T that supports the + operator, demonstrating how generics enhance code reuse.

Generic Structs

Structs can also be parameterized with types, enabling the creation of generic data structures:

```
const Pair = struct(T: type, U: type) {

    first: T,

    second: U,

};
```

```
fn main() void {

    const p = Pair(i32, f32){ .first = 10, .second = 2.5 };

        std.debug.print("Pair: ({}, {})\n", .{p.first, p.second});

}
```

Generic structs make it easy to design versatile and type-safe containers, such as collections or tuples.

Type Inference

Zig's type inference simplifies code by allowing the compiler to deduce types based on context. This feature reduces verbosity without sacrificing clarity or safety.

Inferring Types in Variables

When declaring variables, you can omit the type if the compiler can infer it:

```
pub fn main() void {

    const x = 42; // Inferred as i32

    const y = 3.14; // Inferred as f64

    std.debug.print("x: {}, y: {}\n", .{x, y});

}
```

Inferring Return Types

Zig can also infer the return type of functions, provided it is unambiguous:

```
fn square(x: i32) {

    return x * x; // Type inferred as i32

}


pub fn main() void {

    const result = square(5);

    std.debug.print("Square: {}\n", .{result});

}
```

Type inference streamlines code by reducing redundancy, particularly in scenarios where types are evident from context.

Zig's type system provides developers with the tools to define expressive, maintainable, and efficient code. Through the use of structs, enums, unions, and generics, Zig allows for precise modeling of complex data while maintaining safety and clarity. Combined with features like tagged unions and type inference, Zig strikes a balance between flexibility and control, enabling developers to write high-quality code that is both powerful and intuitive. Whether you're building low-level systems or high-level abstractions, Zig's type system is a reliable and versatile foundation for your projects.

Part 3:

BUILDING REAL-WORLD APPLICATIONS

Part 3 of *this book* marks a significant transition in your journey with Zig. After establishing a strong foundation in the language's core principles and diving deep into its essential features, this section focuses on applying that knowledge to practical, real-world contexts. Here, the theoretical merges with the tangible, enabling you to create robust, performant applications that solve real problems.

The essence of this part lies in understanding how Zig's unique features—like manual memory management, safety mechanisms, and low-level control—translate into practical advantages in application development. Building real-world applications isn't just about writing code that works; it's about designing systems that are efficient, maintainable, and scalable. This section equips you with the tools and strategies to achieve those goals, whether you're building small utilities or large-scale systems.

You'll begin with an exploration of how Zig excels in system-level programming. By learning to develop tools and libraries, you'll see how Zig's philosophy of simplicity and transparency lends itself to high-performance, reusable components. Each chapter emphasizes practical design patterns and techniques, encouraging you to think critically about the decisions that affect the reliability and efficiency of your applications.

As you progress, you'll delve into various application domains where Zig shines. Networking, for example, is a vital focus area. You'll learn to harness Zig's concurrency model and precise control over resources to create scalable, high-speed network applications. From writing simple TCP servers to developing complex communication protocols, this section demonstrates Zig's ability to handle demanding real-world tasks.

Another pivotal topic is file and data processing. Many applications require efficient handling of files, streams, or structured data. This part of the book guides you through creating tools for manipulating data while addressing concerns like performance bottlenecks and memory safety. You'll also explore how Zig can interoperate seamlessly with other systems, making it an excellent choice for projects that demand integration across different languages and platforms.

A highlight of this section is its focus on deployment-ready software. Developing an application is only part of the journey; preparing it for production involves addressing challenges like cross-compilation, error handling, logging, and testing. The book provides practical insights into using Zig's powerful build system to streamline these processes, ensuring your applications are as robust in the field as they are in development.

Finally, the book emphasizes a problem-solving mindset. Real-world applications often come with unique challenges that can't always be anticipated or solved by a one-size-fits-all approach. Through practical examples and hands-on projects, you'll learn to evaluate trade-offs, debug complex issues, and iterate on your designs effectively.

By the end of this part, you'll not only be equipped to build real-world applications with Zig but also gain the confidence to tackle complex development projects head-on, knowing that Zig's performance and simplicity are on your side. This section prepares you to bridge the gap between theory and practice, empowering you to make a meaningful impact in your development work.

8. BUILDING A CLI APPLICATION

Command-line interfaces (CLI) are fundamental tools for developers, system administrators, and power users. They provide a quick, efficient way to perform tasks, often consuming fewer resources than graphical interfaces. In this section, we'll walk through the process of building a CLI application using Zig. Along the way, we'll focus on key aspects like parsing arguments, interacting with files, and communicating with the operating system. This discussion is designed to be practical and informative, enabling you to create your own CLI tools from scratch.

Designing the Foundation of a CLI Application

Building a CLI application begins with defining its purpose and the tasks it will perform. For instance, consider a simple CLI tool that takes a file as input, processes its content (such as counting the number of lines), and outputs the result. This small yet meaningful task gives us a foundation to explore argument parsing, file interaction, and OS communication.

Let's begin with a basic Zig project structure:

Create a new Zig project:

```
zig init-exe my_cli_tool
cd my_cli_tool
```

1. This creates a default `src/main.zig` file, which serves as the entry point for your CLI application.

Modify the `build.zig` file to include meaningful metadata for your project:

```
const std = @import("std");

pub fn build(b: *std.build.Builder) void {

        const exe = b.addExecutable("my_cli_tool",
"src/main.zig");

    exe.setTarget(b.standardTargetOptions(.{}));

    exe.setBuildMode(b.standardReleaseOptions());

    exe.install();

}
```

This setup ensures that your CLI application is well-structured and ready for further development.

PARSING ARGUMENTS

Argument parsing is a core feature of any CLI application. Users pass arguments to specify options, flags, or input values. Zig provides the `std.mem.tokenize` and `std.process.args` utilities to handle command-line arguments.

Here's how you can parse arguments step by step:

Access and tokenize arguments:

```
const std = @import("std");

pub fn main() !void {

                    const args = try
std.process.argsAlloc(std.heap.page_allocator);
```

```
    defer std.process.argsFree(std.heap.page_allocator,
args);


    if (args.len < 2) {

            std.debug.print("Usage:  {}  <file_path>\n",
.{args[0]});

        return;

    }
```

This code retrieves the command-line arguments, checks if a file path is provided, and prints it. The `argsAlloc` function ensures the arguments are allocated correctly in memory.

```
const file_path = args[1];

            std.debug.print("File    to    process:    {}\n",
.{file_path});

}
```

Add flags or options:

 Extend the above program to support optional flags. For example, a -v flag for verbosity:

```
var verbose: bool = false;


for (args[1..]) |arg| {

    if (arg == "-v") {
```

```
        verbose = true;

    } else {

        const file_path = arg;

            std.debug.print("Processing file: {}\n",
.{file_path});

    }

}


if (verbose) {

    std.debug.print("Verbose mode enabled\n", .{});

}
```

1. This example demonstrates a simple way to parse a flag and handle other arguments.

INTERACTING WITH FILES

File interaction is another critical aspect of CLI applications. Zig provides powerful file handling capabilities through `std.fs`.

Reading a file:
Let's extend our CLI to read the content of the file provided by the user.

```
pub fn main() !void {
```

```zig
    const allocator = std.heap.page_allocator;

    const args = try std.process.argsAlloc(allocator);

    defer std.process.argsFree(allocator, args);


    if (args.len < 2) {

            std.debug.print("Usage: {} <file_path>\n",
.{args[0]});

        return;

    }


    const file_path = args[1];

     const file = try std.fs.cwd().openFile(file_path,
.{ .read = true });

    defer file.close();


    const content = try file.readToEnd(allocator);

    defer allocator.free(content);


            std.debug.print("File    content:\n{any}\n",
.{content});

}
```

This example reads the file content into memory and prints it. The `std.fs.cwd().openFile` method ensures that the file is opened relative to the current working directory.

Writing to a file:
To extend functionality, you may want your CLI to write output to a file:

```
const output_file = try
std.fs.cwd().createFile("output.txt", .{ .truncate =
true });

defer output_file.close();


try output_file.write("This is the output.\n");

std.debug.print("Output written to output.txt\n", .{});
```

1. This snippet writes the string "This is the output." to a file named `output.txt`.

Interacting with the Operating System

Zig provides system-level APIs to communicate with the operating system, which can be invaluable for CLI applications that need to spawn processes, manipulate the environment, or perform other system-specific tasks.

Spawning a subprocess:

You can invoke other commands or scripts using `std.process.spawn`:

```
const command = std.process.spawn(.{

    .argv = &[_][]const u8{"ls", "-la"},

}) catch |err| {

    std.debug.print("Failed to execute command: {}\n",
.{err});

    return;

};



defer command.deinit();



const stdout_stream = command.stdout_stream.?;

while (try stdout_stream.readToEnd(allocator)) |line| {

    std.debug.print("{}", .{line});

}
```

This example runs the `ls -la` command (list directory contents) and prints its output.

Setting environment variables:
Sometimes, CLI applications modify the environment for subprocesses or other tasks:

```
std.process.setEnvVar("MY_ENV_VAR",          "some_value",
.overwrite);

std.debug.print("Environment        variable        set:
MY_ENV_VAR={}\n", .{"some_value"});
```

Use this to control the environment context for your CLI or spawned processes.

Complete CLI Application Example

To tie these concepts together, here's a complete example of a CLI application that counts the number of lines in a file, supports a verbosity flag, and writes the result to an output file:

```
const std = @import("std");

pub fn main() !void {

    const allocator = std.heap.page_allocator;

    const args = try std.process.argsAlloc(allocator);

    defer std.process.argsFree(allocator, args);


    if (args.len < 2) {

        std.debug.print("Usage: {} [-v] <file_path>\n",
.{args[0]});

        return;
```

```zig
    }


    var verbose: bool = false;

    var file_path: ?[]const u8 = null;


    for (args[1..]) |arg| {

        if (arg == "-v") {

            verbose = true;

        } else {

            file_path = arg;

        }

    }


    if (file_path == null) {

                std.debug.print("Error:  File  path  is
required.\n", .{});

        return;

    }
```

```
    const file = try std.fs.cwd().openFile(file_path.?,
.{ .read = true });

    defer file.close();


    const content = try file.readToEnd(allocator);

    defer allocator.free(content);


        const line_count = std.mem.tokenize(content,
"\n").len;

    if (verbose) {

        std.debug.print("Verbose: File has {} lines\n",
.{line_count});

    }


                const output_file = try
std.fs.cwd().createFile("output.txt", .{ .truncate =
true });

    defer output_file.close();


        try output_file.writeFmt("Line count: {}\n",
.{line_count});
```

```
    std.debug.print("Result written to output.txt\n",
.{});

}
```

Building CLI

applications in Zig is a rewarding experience because of the language's focus on performance, simplicity, and safety. By mastering argument parsing, file interaction, and OS communication, you can create powerful tools that address real-world challenges. The example above combines all these elements into a practical, reusable framework for further exploration. Use this as a starting point to build more complex and specialized applications tailored to your needs.

9. DEVELOPING A NETWORKING APPLICATION

Networking applications form the backbone of modern computing, powering everything from simple chat apps to complex distributed systems. Zig, with its low-level control and performance-oriented design, is an excellent choice for building networking applications. In this discussion, we'll explore how to develop a networking application by working with sockets, understanding protocols, and handling concurrency effectively. By the end, you'll have a solid foundation to create your own efficient and scalable networked systems.

Understanding the Basics of Networking in Zig

Networking involves communication between systems using protocols and sockets. At its core, a socket acts as an endpoint for sending and receiving data over a network. Protocols like TCP (Transmission Control Protocol) and UDP (User Datagram Protocol) define the rules for communication.

To create a networking application, we'll use Zig's `std.net` module, which provides tools to work with sockets, handle connections, and manage data transfers.

SOCKETS AND PROTOCOLS

Let's start by creating a basic TCP server and client. TCP is a reliable, connection-oriented protocol that ensures data delivery.

Creating a TCP Server
A TCP server listens for incoming connections, accepts them, and processes requests from clients. Here's how you can implement a simple TCP server in Zig:

This server listens on port `8080` and sends a greeting message to any

```zig
const std = @import("std");

pub fn main() !void {

    const allocator = std.heap.page_allocator;

    // Create a TCP listener socket
    const listener = try std.net.tcpListen(std.net.Address.parseIp4("0.0.0.0", 8080));
    defer listener.close();

    std.debug.print("Server listening on 0.0.0.0:8080...\n", .{});

    while (true) {

        const conn = try listener.accept();

        defer conn.close();

        std.debug.print("Accepted connection from {any}\n", .{conn.peer.address});

        try conn.writeAll("Hello from Zig server!\n");
```

```
        }

}
```

client that connects.

Creating a TCP Client
A client connects to the server and exchanges data. Here's a simple implementation:

```
pub fn main() !void {

    const allocator = std.heap.page_allocator;


    // Connect to the server
                        const     conn     =     try
std.net.tcpConnect(std.net.Address.parseIp4("127.0.0.1"
, 8080));

    defer conn.close();


    const buffer = try conn.readToEndAlloc(allocator);

    defer allocator.free(buffer);


        std.debug.print("Server   response:   {any}\n",
.{buffer});

}
```

The client connects to `127.0.0.1:8080`, reads the server's response, and prints it.

HANDLING CONCURRENCY IN NETWORKED SYSTEMS

Concurrency is essential in networking to handle multiple clients simultaneously without blocking the entire system. Zig's approach to concurrency involves cooperative multitasking using `async` and `await`.

Asynchronous TCP Server
Modify the server to handle multiple connections concurrently using Zig's `async` feature:

```
const std = @import("std");


pub fn main() !void {

    const allocator = std.heap.page_allocator;

                    const    listener    =    try
std.net.tcpListen(std.net.Address.parseIp4("0.0.0.0",
8080));

    defer listener.close();



        std.debug.print("Async    server    listening    on
0.0.0.0:8080...\n", .{});



    while (true) {
```

```
    const conn = try listener.accept();

    async handleClient(conn);

  }

}


pub fn handleClient(conn: std.net.StreamServer) !void {

    defer conn.close();

                        const     buffer   =      try
conn.readToEndAlloc(std.heap.page_allocator);

    defer std.heap.page_allocator.free(buffer);


    std.debug.print("Received: {any}\n", .{buffer});

    try conn.writeAll("Response from server\n");

}
```

Each client connection is processed in a separate async task, allowing the server to handle multiple clients without blocking.

Concurrency in Clients

If the client needs to perform tasks like downloading multiple files or handling parallel connections, you can use async to manage concurrent tasks:

```
pub fn main() !void {

    var tasks = [_]async void {
```

```zig
        downloadFile("127.0.0.1", 8080, "file1.txt"),

        downloadFile("127.0.0.1", 8080, "file2.txt"),

    };


    for (tasks) |*task| {

        await task;

    }

}


pub fn downloadFile(ip: []const u8, port: u16,
filename: []const u8) !void {

                    const conn        =       try
std.net.tcpConnect(std.net.Address.parseIp4(ip, port));

    defer conn.close();


    try conn.writeAll("GET " ++ filename ++ "\n");

                const response     =       try
conn.readToEndAlloc(std.heap.page_allocator);

    defer std.heap.page_allocator.free(response);
```

```
        std.debug.print("Downloaded    {}:    {any}\n",
.{filename, response});

}
```

This example concurrently downloads two files from the server, showcasing how `async` simplifies managing parallel tasks.

Advanced Networking Features

Beyond basic sockets, Zig's networking API supports advanced use cases.

UDP Communication

UDP is a lightweight, connectionless protocol. Here's an example of a simple UDP server and client:

UDP Server

```
pub fn main() !void {

    const socket = try std.net.udpSocket();

    defer socket.close();


    try socket.bind(std.net.Address.parseIp4("0.0.0.0",
8080));

        std.debug.print("UDP   server   listening   on
0.0.0.0:8080...\n", .{});
```

```zig
    var buffer: [128]u8 = undefined;

    while (true) {

        const sender = try socket.receiveFrom(&buffer);

        std.debug.print("Received from {any}: {any}\n",
.{sender.address, buffer});

        try socket.sendTo(sender.address, "Ack from
server\n");

    }

}
```

UDP Client

```zig
pub fn main() !void {

    const socket = try std.net.udpSocket();

    defer socket.close();


            const         server_addr        =
std.net.Address.parseIp4("127.0.0.1", 8080);

        try  socket.sendTo(server_addr,  "Hello,  UDP
server!\n");


    var buffer: [128]u8 = undefined;

    const sender = try socket.receiveFrom(&buffer);
```

```
        std.debug.print("Response from {any}: {any}\n",
.{sender.address, buffer});
```

```
}
```

1. **TLS Communication**

   For secure communication, Zig supports TLS via third-party
   libraries or the standard library (if linked with OpenSSL or
   BoringSSL). Setting up TLS involves wrapping a TCP connection
   with a secure layer, ensuring data confidentiality and integrity.

Complete Networking Application Example

Let's combine these elements into a simple chat server and client.

Chat Server

```
const std = @import("std");


pub fn main() !void {
                const      listener      =      try
std.net.tcpListen(std.net.Address.parseIp4("0.0.0.0",
8080));

    defer listener.close();


    while (true) {

        const conn = try listener.accept();

        async handleClient(conn);
```

```
    }

}


pub fn handleClient(conn: std.net.StreamServer) !void {

    defer conn.close();

    var buffer: [128]u8 = undefined;


    while (true) {

                        const    bytes_read   =    try
conn.reader.read(&buffer);

            if (bytes_read == 0) break; // Connection
closed

                                                    try
conn.writer.writeAll(buffer[0..bytes_read]);

    }

}
```

Chat Client

```
const std = @import("std");


pub fn main() !void {
```

```
                    const    conn    =    try
std.net.tcpConnect(std.net.Address.parseIp4("127.0.0.1"
, 8080));

    defer conn.close();


    const stdin = std.io.getStdIn();

    const stdout = std.io.getStdOut();


    async {

        var buffer: [128]u8 = undefined;

        while (true) {

                        const  bytes_read  =  try
conn.reader.read(&buffer);

            if (bytes_read == 0) break;

                                            try
stdout.writer().writeAll(buffer[0..bytes_read]);

        }

    };


    var input: [128]u8 = undefined;

    while (true) {
```

```
                    const    bytes_read    =    try
stdin.reader().read(&input);

        if (bytes_read == 0) break;

        try conn.writer.writeAll(input[0..bytes_read]);

    }

}
```

This basic chat system highlights how to use sockets, manage data flow, and handle concurrency effectively.

Networking in Zig is both efficient and elegant, thanks to its powerful standard library and straightforward concurrency model. By understanding sockets, protocols, and concurrency, you can build scalable and robust networked systems tailored to your requirements. Use these examples as building blocks to create more advanced applications, such as HTTP servers, real-time systems, or distributed databases.

CREATING A HIGH-PERFORMANCE LIBRARY

Developing a high-performance library is a rewarding challenge that requires a balance of careful design, optimization, and modularity. Libraries are meant to solve problems in a reusable way, which demands not only correctness but also speed, memory efficiency, and maintainability. Zig's performance-oriented design and lightweight abstractions make it an excellent choice for building such libraries.

In this discussion, we'll focus on creating a high-performance library by optimizing for speed and memory efficiency while ensuring the library remains reusable and modular.

Designing a High-Performance Library

Before diving into implementation, take time to design the library. A well-designed library focuses on:

- **A Clear API**: Define an intuitive interface that developers can easily understand and use.
- **Performance Goals**: Identify key metrics, such as speed and memory usage, to guide optimization.
- **Modularity**: Break the library into reusable, independent components.

For this example, let's create a library for efficient string searching using the Boyer-Moore algorithm—a widely used algorithm optimized for speed.

OPTIMIZING FOR SPEED AND MEMORY EFFICIENCY

The Boyer-Moore algorithm is chosen for its ability to skip sections of the input string, making it faster than naive string search methods. Here's how to implement and optimize it:

1. **Efficient Data Structures**
   Use precomputed lookup tables to minimize redundant computation. For the Boyer-Moore algorithm, a "bad character table" and a "good suffix table" are commonly used.

2. **Memory Allocation**
   Avoid frequent dynamic memory allocation. Zig allows you to work directly with slices and stack-allocated buffers, reducing overhead.

Implementation

Here's the implementation of the Boyer-Moore search algorithm:

```zig
const std = @import("std");


pub fn boyerMooreSearch(haystack: []const u8, needle: []const u8) ?usize {

    if (needle.len == 0) return null;

    if (needle.len > haystack.len) return null;


    // Build the bad character table

    var bad_char_table: [256]usize = undefined;

    for (bad_char_table) |*entry| entry.* = needle.len;

    for (needle[0..needle.len - 1]) |c, i| {
```

```
        bad_char_table[c] = needle.len - i - 1;

    }


    var i: usize = needle.len - 1;

    while (i < haystack.len) {

        var j: usize = needle.len - 1;

            while (haystack[i - (needle.len - 1 - j)] ==
needle[j]) {

                if (j == 0) return i - (needle.len - 1);

                j -= 1;

            }

        i += bad_char_table[haystack[i]];

    }


    return null;

}
```

3. **Bad Character Table**: This table is precomputed to store how far
   the algorithm can skip when a mismatch occurs.

   Memory Efficiency: The algorithm operates in-place on the
   haystack and needle slices, avoiding unnecessary allocations.

Benchmarking for Speed

Zig's standard library includes benchmarking utilities. To measure the performance of your library, write benchmarks:

```
pub fn benchmark() !void {

    const std = @import("std");

    var timer = std.time.Timer.start();


    const haystack = "this is a sample text for
benchmarking";

    const needle = "sample";


    _ = boyerMooreSearch(haystack, needle);

    const elapsed = timer.end();

            std.debug.print("Elapsed   time:   {}ns\n",
.{elapsed});

}
```

This function measures the time taken to perform a search, providing insights into performance improvements.

WRITING REUSABLE MODULES

Modularity is key to a successful library. A reusable module should focus on:

1. **Encapsulation**
   Hide implementation details and expose only necessary functions

or types.

2. **Generic Interfaces**
   Allow your module to work with various data types or contexts without significant changes.

Here's how to refactor the Boyer-Moore algorithm into a reusable module:

Module Structure

Create a separate file, `string_search.zig`:

```
const std = @import("std");


pub fn boyerMooreSearch(haystack: []const u8, needle:
[]const u8) ?usize {

    if (needle.len == 0) return null;

    if (needle.len > haystack.len) return null;


    var bad_char_table: [256]usize = undefined;

    for (bad_char_table) |*entry| entry.* = needle.len;

    for (needle[0..needle.len - 1]) |c, i| {

        bad_char_table[c] = needle.len - i - 1;

    }
```

```
    var i: usize = needle.len - 1;

    while (i < haystack.len) {

        var j: usize = needle.len - 1;

            while (haystack[i - (needle.len - 1 - j)] ==
needle[j]) {

                if (j == 0) return i - (needle.len - 1);

                j -= 1;

        }

        i += bad_char_table[haystack[i]];

    }


    return null;

}
```

Testing the Module

Use Zig's built-in testing framework to ensure your module works correctly:

```
const string_search = @import("string_search");


test "Boyer-Moore search works correctly" {
```

```zig
    const haystack = "this is a simple example";

    const needle = "simple";

    const result =
string_search.boyerMooreSearch(haystack, needle);

    try std.testing.expect(result == 10);
```

Using the Module in Applications

Import the module into another Zig file to use it in different contexts:

```zig
const string_search = @import("string_search");


pub fn main() !void {
    const haystack = "look for the substring in this
text";

    const needle = "substring";


    const result =
string_search.boyerMooreSearch(haystack, needle);

    if (result) |index| {

        std.debug.print("Substring found at index
{}\n", .{index});

    } else {
```

```
    std.debug.print("Substring not found.\n", .{});

    }

}
```

This modular structure allows the library to be reused across multiple projects.

Optimizing Further

Parallelization

For larger inputs, consider using Zig's async to parallelize the search:

```
pub fn parallelSearch(haystack: []const u8, needle:
[]const u8) ?usize {

    const chunk_size = haystack.len / 4; // Divide into
4 chunks

    var tasks = [_]async ?usize {

        searchChunk(haystack[0..chunk_size], needle),

        searchChunk(haystack[chunk_size..2*chunk_size],
needle),

searchChunk(haystack[2*chunk_size..3*chunk_size],
needle),

        searchChunk(haystack[3*chunk_size..], needle),

    };
```

```
for (tasks) |*task| {

    const result = await task;

    if (result) return result;

}

return null;

}


pub fn searchChunk(haystack: []const u8, needle:
[]const u8) ?usize {

    return boyerMooreSearch(haystack, needle);

}
```

This splits the haystack into chunks and searches them concurrently.

1. **Custom Memory Allocators**
   Optimize memory allocation by providing custom allocators
   tailored to your use case, reducing overhead in memory-intensive
   operations.

Creating a high-performance library in Zig is about leveraging its strengths: low-level control, performance-oriented design, and safety features. By optimizing for speed and memory efficiency, writing modular code, and employing reusable components, you can build libraries that are not only fast but also widely applicable. The Boyer-Moore example illustrates how to balance these elements, giving you a practical foundation for tackling more complex library projects.

11. INTERFACING WITH C AND OTHER LANGUAGES

Zig is designed to seamlessly interface with other programming languages, especially C. This interoperability is achieved through its Foreign Function Interface (FFI), allowing developers to call C functions, use C libraries, and integrate Zig code into existing projects. By understanding Zig's interop capabilities, you can unlock new opportunities to reuse legacy code, enhance libraries, and integrate with diverse ecosystems.

This discussion will cover the principles of FFI, interop with C libraries, and practical examples to help you integrate Zig with other languages effectively.

Why Interfacing Matters

Interfacing with C and other languages is crucial for:

1. **Reusing Code**: Many well-established libraries (e.g., OpenSSL, SQLite) are written in C. Interfacing allows Zig programs to leverage these libraries without rewriting them.
2. **Extending Zig Applications**: Use external libraries for tasks Zig's standard library doesn't natively support.
3. **Adopting Zig Gradually**: Incrementally migrate C projects to Zig while maintaining functionality.

Interop with C Libraries

Zig's ability to work with C libraries comes from its built-in support for C headers and ABI (Application Binary Interface) compatibility.

Importing C Headers

Zig can directly parse and import C headers using `@cImport`. This eliminates the need for manual function declarations. For example, to use the `math.h` functions:

```
const std = @import("std");
```

```
const c = @cImport(@cInclude("math.h"));
```

```
pub fn main() void {
    const result = c.sqrt(16.0);
        std.debug.print("Square  root  of  16  is  {}\n",
.{result});
}
```

- o `@cImport`: Allows importing C headers directly.
- o `@cInclude`: Specifies the required C header.
2. Ensure that the required headers are available in the system's standard include paths.

Calling a C Function

Zig can call any C function as long as you provide the correct type definitions. For example, integrating a simple C function:

C Code (`example.c`):

```
#include <stdio.h>
```

```c
void greet(const char *name) {

    printf("Hello, %s!\n", name);

}
```

Zig Code (`main.zig`):

```zig
const std = @import("std");


extern fn greet(name: [*:0]const u8) void;


pub fn main() void {

    greet("Zig");

}
```

- `extern fn`: Declares an external C function.
- The `name` parameter in the C function corresponds to Zig's `[*:0]const u8` type, representing a null-terminated string.

Linking C Libraries

To use compiled C libraries, specify the `.so`, `.dll`, or `.a` file during Zig's build process.

Build file (`build.zig`):
```zig
const Builder = @import("std").build.Builder;
```

```
pub fn build(b: *Builder) void {

    const exe = b.addExecutable("interop-example",
"src/main.zig");

    exe.linkSystemLibrary("m"); // Link math library

    exe.setTarget(b.standardTargetOptions(.{}));

    exe.setBuildMode(b.standardReleaseOptions());

    exe.install();

}
```

This links Zig with the `math` library. For custom libraries, replace `"m"` with the library name.

FFI Principles

FFI is the mechanism that enables Zig to call functions and use data structures from other languages. Understanding these principles ensures smooth interoperation:

1. **ABI Compatibility**
   Zig's ABI is compatible with C, meaning structures, functions, and types align directly. Ensure that function signatures and data types match between Zig and the foreign language.

2. **Data Type Mapping**
   Zig provides equivalents for C types. Examples:

C Type	Zig Type
int	c_int
float	f32
char *	[*:0]const u8
void *	?*anyopaque

3.
   Use Zig's @cImport to avoid manual mapping errors.

4. **Memory Management**

   ○ C libraries often allocate memory dynamically, requiring
     manual deallocation.
   ○ Use Zig's allocators to manage memory efficiently. For
     example:

```
const allocator = std.heap.page_allocator;


var buffer = try allocator.alloc(u8, 100);

defer allocator.free(buffer);
```

Practical Example: Integrating a SQLite Database

Let's integrate the SQLite C library with Zig to perform database operations.

1. **Install SQLite**
   Ensure SQLite is installed on your system (`libsqlite3` on Linux/macOS or `sqlite3.dll` on Windows).

Write the Zig Code

```zig
const std = @import("std");

const c = @cImport(@cInclude("sqlite3.h"));

pub fn main() !void {
    const db_ptr = try openDatabase("example.db");
    defer closeDatabase(db_ptr);


    try executeQuery(db_ptr, "CREATE TABLE IF NOT EXISTS users (id INTEGER PRIMARY KEY, name TEXT);");

    try executeQuery(db_ptr, "INSERT INTO users (name) VALUES ('Alice');");
```

```
        std.debug.print("Database operations completed
successfully.\n", .{});
}


fn openDatabase(filename: []const u8) !*c.sqlite3 {
    var db: ?*c.sqlite3 = null;
    const rc = c.sqlite3_open(filename, &db);
    if (rc != c.SQLITE_OK) return error.DatabaseError;
    return db;
}


fn closeDatabase(db: *c.sqlite3) void {
    _ = c.sqlite3_close(db);
}


fn executeQuery(db: *c.sqlite3, query: []const u8)
!void {
    const rc = c.sqlite3_exec(db, query, null, null,
null);
    if (rc != c.SQLITE_OK) return error.QueryError;
```

```
}
```

- o The `@cImport` directive imports `sqlite3.h` directly.
- o The `openDatabase`, `closeDatabase`, and `executeQuery` functions wrap SQLite C functions for Zig usage.
- o Errors are handled using Zig's `error` system.

Build the Project

Use a `build.zig` file to link SQLite:

```
const Builder = @import("std").build.Builder;


pub fn build(b: *Builder) void {
        const  exe  =  b.addExecutable("sqlite-example",
"src/main.zig");

    exe.linkSystemLibrary("sqlite3");

    exe.setBuildMode(b.standardReleaseOptions());

    exe.install();
}
```

Run the application using `zig build run`.

Interfacing with Other Languages

Although Zig excels at interop with C, it can also interface with other languages via FFI wrappers or bridges:

Calling Zig from C

Export Zig functions as C-compatible using the `export` keyword:

```
export fn add(a: c_int, b: c_int) c_int {

    return a + b;

}.
```

Compile the Zig code to a shared library (`.so`, `.dll`, or `.dylib`) and call it from C.

1. **Interfacing with Rust**

   Use Zig's ABI compatibility with C to bridge Rust and Zig code. Compile Zig functions into shared libraries and link them in Rust using `extern "C"`.

Zig's seamless FFI support empowers developers to integrate powerful C libraries, extend applications with Zig, and interoperate with other ecosystems. By following the principles of ABI compatibility, type mapping, and memory management, you can confidently build robust, interoperable systems. The SQLite example demonstrates how easy it is to leverage Zig's FFI for practical, real-world tasks, paving the way for more ambitious integrations.

12. ZIG FOR SYSTEMS PROGRAMMING

Zig is designed with systems programming in mind, providing developers with precise control over memory, low-level features, and minimal runtime overhead. Its design philosophy emphasizes safety without sacrificing performance, making it an excellent choice for tasks like bare-metal programming and custom memory management. In this discussion, we'll explore the basics of bare-metal programming and delve into writing a custom allocator in Zig.

Why Zig for Systems Programming?

Systems programming involves developing low-level software that interacts directly with hardware or provides foundational services for higher-level applications. Zig excels in this domain because of its:

1. **Predictable Behavior**: Zig avoids hidden control flow (e.g., implicit exceptions) and minimizes runtime dependencies.
2. **Fine-grained Memory Control**: Zig enables precise control over memory allocation and deallocation.
3. **Cross-compilation**: Zig has first-class support for cross-compiling, essential for embedded or bare-metal development.
4. **Minimal Dependencies**: Zig's standard library is optional, which is crucial for environments with strict memory or storage constraints.

BARE-METAL PROGRAMMING BASICS

Bare-metal programming refers to writing software that runs directly on hardware without an operating system. This requires understanding the hardware architecture, managing peripherals, and handling interrupts. Zig is well-suited for such tasks due to its lightweight nature and low-level capabilities.

Setting Up a Bare-metal Environment

To begin, define the target architecture and configure the toolchain. Zig provides built-in cross-compilation capabilities, eliminating the need for external tools.

For example, to target an ARM Cortex-M microcontroller:

```
zig build-exe --target-arm --mcpu=cortex-m4 main.zig
```

This compiles your Zig program for an ARM Cortex-M4 processor.

Minimal Bare-metal Program

A bare-metal program typically starts at the reset vector and executes without relying on any operating system services. Here's a minimal example:

```
const std = @import("std");



// Entry point

pub export fn _start() noreturn {

        const led_port = @intToPtr(*volatile u32, 0x40020C14); // GPIO port address

    led_port.* = 0x01; // Turn on the LED

    while (true) {}

}
```

- The `_start` function serves as the entry point, replacing the default `main` function.
- `@intToPtr`: Converts a memory address to a pointer.
- `*volatile`: Ensures the compiler doesn't optimize out hardware access.

Accessing Peripherals

Hardware peripherals are accessed via memory-mapped registers. Zig's low-level control makes this straightforward:

```
const uart_base = @intToPtr(*volatile u32, 0x40013800);
// UART base address
```

```
pub fn write_uart(data: u8) void {
    const uart_dr = uart_base + 0x04; // Data register offset

    uart_dr.* = data;
}
```

- Peripherals are typically represented as memory-mapped regions, accessed using their base addresses.

Interrupt Handling

Zig supports defining interrupt handlers using the `export` keyword:

```
pub export fn SysTick_Handler() void {
```

```
    // Handle system tick interrupt

}
```

This function is automatically called when the corresponding interrupt occurs, depending on your microcontroller's vector table configuration.

WRITING A CUSTOM ALLOCATOR

Custom memory allocators are vital for systems programming, especially in constrained environments like embedded systems or custom kernels. A custom allocator allows you to define how memory is allocated, reused, and freed, tailored to your application's specific needs.

1. **Understanding Zig's Allocator Interface**

   Zig provides a standardized `Allocator` interface, which defines methods like:

   - `alloc`: Allocates memory.
   - `resize`: Resizes an existing allocation.
   - `free`: Deallocates memory.

Here's the structure of a custom allocator:
```
const std = @import("std");


pub const MyAllocator = struct {

    mem: []u8, // Memory pool
```

```
    next: usize, // Next free location


    pub fn init(pool: []u8) MyAllocator {

        return MyAllocator{ .mem = pool, .next = 0 };

    }



    pub fn alloc(self: *MyAllocator, comptime T: type,
count: usize) ![]T {

        const needed = @sizeOf(T) * count;

        if (self.next + needed > self.mem.len) return
error.OutOfMemory;

        const start = self.next;

        self.next += needed;

        return self.mem[start..start + needed][0..:T];

    }



    pub fn free(self: *MyAllocator, _: []anytype) void
{

        // Simple allocator does not support freeing

    }
};
```

- The allocator uses a pre-allocated memory pool (mem).
- Allocations are sequential, making this allocator suitable for fixed-size buffers or temporary allocations.

Using the Custom Allocator

Initialize and use the custom allocator:

```
const std = @import("std");

const                      MyAllocator                      =
@import("my_allocator").MyAllocator;


pub fn main() !void {

    var pool: [1024]u8 = undefined;

    var allocator = MyAllocator.init(&pool);


    const buffer = try allocator.alloc(u8, 256);

    std.debug.print("Allocated 256 bytes.\n", .{});
}
```

- The buffer is allocated from the memory pool.
- If the pool lacks sufficient space, the allocator returns an OutOfMemory error.

2. **Adding Advanced Features**

Enhance the custom allocator for more functionality:

- **Freeing Memory**: Implement a free list to reclaim memory.
- **Defragmentation**: Compact memory to avoid fragmentation in long-running systems.

Example of a free-list allocator:

```
pub const FreeListAllocator = struct {

    free_list: ?*Node,

    mem: []u8,


    pub fn init(pool: []u8) FreeListAllocator {

        return FreeListAllocator{ .free_list = null,
.mem = pool };

    }


    pub fn alloc(self: *FreeListAllocator, comptime T:
type, count: usize) ![]T {

        // Implementation of allocation with free list

    }


    pub fn free(self: *FreeListAllocator, ptr: []u8)
void {

        // Add memory back to the free list

    }
```

```
    const Node = struct {

        next: ?*Node,

    };

};
```

- o The Node structure tracks free blocks of memory.
- o The alloc and free methods interact with the free list to allocate and reclaim memory.

Practical Use Case: Memory Pool for Embedded Systems

For embedded systems, memory pools are often used to allocate objects of fixed sizes efficiently. Here's how to create a memory pool allocator:

```
const std = @import("std");

pub const MemoryPool = struct {
    pool: []u8,
    block_size: usize,
    free_list: ?*Node,

    pub fn init(pool: []u8, block_size: usize)
MemoryPool {
        return MemoryPool{ .pool = pool, .block_size =
block_size, .free_list = null };
    }

    pub fn alloc(self: *MemoryPool) ?*u8 {
```

```
        if (self.free_list) |free_block| {
            self.free_list = free_block.next;
            return @intToPtr(*u8, free_block);
        }
        if (self.pool.len < self.block_size) return
null;
        const block = &self.pool[0..self.block_size];
        self.pool = self.pool[self.block_size..];
        return block.ptr;
    }

    pub fn free(self: *MemoryPool, block: *u8) void {
        self.free_list = &Node{ .next = self.free_list
};
        @memcpy(self.free_list, block,
self.block_size);
    }

    const Node = struct {
        next: ?*Node,
    };
};
```

- The allocator divides a memory pool into fixed-size blocks.
- Freed blocks are added back to the free list for reuse.

Zig's focus on performance, safety, and minimalism makes it an exceptional tool for systems programming. Whether you're developing bare-metal applications or implementing custom memory allocators, Zig provides the flexibility and control needed for low-level tasks. The examples here provide a foundation for building efficient and reliable systems while leveraging Zig's powerful features.

13. DEBUGGING AND PROFILING ZIG APPLICATIONS

Efficient debugging and profiling are critical for building robust and high-performance applications. Zig's design emphasizes clarity and simplicity, which naturally aids debugging and performance tuning. Furthermore, Zig integrates seamlessly with existing debugging and profiling tools, allowing developers to leverage these capabilities while taking advantage of Zig's specific features. In this discussion, we'll explore debugging tools and techniques, as well as profiling and performance tuning in Zig.

DEBUGGING TOOLS AND TECHNIQUES

Debugging is the process of identifying and fixing errors in a program. Zig provides several ways to debug applications, from compiler features to external tools.

1. Using Zig's Built-in Debugging Features

Debug Build Mode:
 Zig offers different build modes, and the Debug mode includes extra checks and debugging symbols to make debugging easier.

```
zig build -Drelease-safe=false
```

- In Debug mode, Zig inserts runtime safety checks, such as:

  - Bounds checking for arrays.
  - Detection of null pointer dereferences.
  - Overflow checks for integer operations.

Standard Library Debugging Functions:
The Zig standard library provides tools to print runtime information, such as variables and execution flow.

This outputs the value of x to the console, useful for inspecting variables during execution.

2. Leveraging External Debuggers

GDB (GNU Debugger):
Zig is compatible with GDB, a powerful tool for inspecting program execution. Use GDB to set breakpoints, step through code, and examine memory.

```
const std = @import("std");


pub fn main() void {

    const x = 42;

    std.debug.print("Value of x: {}\n", .{x});

}
```
Compile your program with debugging symbols:

Key GDB commands:
```
zig build-exe -g main.zig
```

```
 Run the program in GDB:



 gdb ./main
```

- o `break <line_number>`: Sets a breakpoint at a specific line.
- o `run`: Starts the program.
- o `next` / `step`: Steps through the code.
- o `print <variable>`: Displays the value of a variable.

LLDB (LLVM Debugger):
LLDB, similar to GDB, works well with Zig. To use LLDB:

lldb ./main

- Follow similar commands as GDB (`break`, `run`, `step`, etc.).

3. Debugging Memory Issues

Zig's manual memory management makes it prone to common issues like memory leaks or undefined behavior. Tools like **Valgrind** can help detect these:

valgrind ./main

Valgrind reports invalid memory access, leaks, and undefined behavior, aiding debugging in complex systems.

PROFILING AND PERFORMANCE TUNING

Profiling is the process of analyzing a program's runtime performance, including identifying bottlenecks, optimizing resource usage, and improving efficiency. Zig's minimal runtime and predictable behavior make it easier to tune performance.

1. Compile with Performance in Mind

Zig supports multiple build modes optimized for performance:

- **ReleaseFast**: Optimized for speed.
- **ReleaseSmall**: Optimized for binary size.

zig build -Drelease-fast=true

Release modes enable aggressive compiler optimizations, such as inlining and loop unrolling, for faster execution.

2. Profiling with External Tools

perf (Linux):
`perf` is a powerful Linux profiling tool that records CPU usage, cache misses, and other performance metrics.

Use `perf` with Zig:

perf record ./main

perf report

- The `perf report` command provides detailed insights into which functions consume the most CPU time.
- **Instruments (macOS)**:
  On macOS, Instruments can profile Zig applications for performance bottlenecks, memory leaks, and more. Open your Zig binary in Instruments and run the profiling tools.
- **Visual Studio Profiler (Windows)**:
  On Windows, you can use Visual Studio's built-in profiling tools to measure performance, memory, and threading issues in Zig

applications.

3. Timing Code Execution

Measure execution time directly in Zig to find slow sections:

```
const std = @import("std");

pub fn main() void {
    var timer = std.time.timer();
    const start = timer.timestamp();


    // Code to profile
    std.debug.print("Hello, Zig!\n", .{});


    const end = timer.timestamp();
    std.debug.print("Execution time: {} ns\n", .{end -
start});
}
```

- This example measures the time (in nanoseconds) a code block takes to execute.
- Use this method to identify hotspots in your code.

4. Optimizing Performance

Once profiling identifies bottlenecks, optimize your code with these strategies:

- **Memory Optimization**:
  Avoid unnecessary allocations and use custom allocators where possible. For example, a stack allocator can improve performance in scenarios where memory is allocated and freed in a LIFO manner.

- **Algorithm Optimization**:
  Replace inefficient algorithms with more optimized ones. For instance, use binary search instead of linear search for sorted data.

Concurrency:
Exploit Zig's support for multi-threading to parallelize workloads. For example:

```
const std = @import("std");


pub fn main() !void {

    var t1 = try std.Thread.spawn(fn() void {

        std.debug.print("Thread 1 running\n", .{});

    });

    defer t1.join();
```

```
var t2 = try std.Thread.spawn(fn() void {

    std.debug.print("Thread 2 running\n", .{});

});

defer t2.join();

}
```

This spawns two threads to perform tasks concurrently, reducing execution time.

5. Inline Assembly for Critical Sections

For maximum performance in systems programming, Zig allows embedding assembly code for critical sections:

```
pub fn fast_add(a: u32, b: u32) u32 {

    return asm volatile ("add {0}, {1}, {2}" : [result]
"=r" (u32) : [op1] "r" (a), [op2] "r" (b));

}
```

This example uses ARM assembly to perform addition, useful for performance-critical applications.

Practical Example: Profiling and Optimizing a Sorting Algorithm

Let's profile and optimize a sorting algorithm in Zig:

1. **Initial Implementation**

```
const std = @import("std");
```

```
pub fn bubbleSort(arr: []u32) void {

    for (arr) |_, i| {

        for (arr[0..arr.len - i - 1]) |_, j| {

            if (arr[j] > arr[j + 1]) {

                const temp = arr[j];

                arr[j] = arr[j + 1];

                arr[j + 1] = temp;

            }

        }

    }

}
```

2. **Profiling the Code**

Compile the program in Debug mode and profile it using `perf` or Instruments. The profiling report will likely show that `bubbleSort` takes a significant amount of time for large arrays.

3. **Optimized Implementation**

Replace the bubble sort with a more efficient algorithm, such as quicksort:

```
pub fn quickSort(arr: []u32, lo: usize, hi: usize) void
{

    if (lo < hi) {
```

```
        const p = partition(arr, lo, hi);

        quickSort(arr, lo, p - 1);

        quickSort(arr, p + 1, hi);

    }

}


fn partition(arr: []u32, lo: usize, hi: usize) usize {

    const pivot = arr[hi];

    var i = lo;

    for (arr[lo..hi]) |_, j| {

        if (arr[j] < pivot) {

            const temp = arr[i];

            arr[i] = arr[j];

            arr[j] = temp;

            i += 1;

        }

    }

    const temp = arr[i];

    arr[i] = arr[hi];
```

```
    arr[hi] = temp;

    return i;

}
```

This implementation is significantly faster, as profiling will demonstrate.

Debugging and profiling are integral to building reliable, high-performance applications in Zig. By leveraging Zig's built-in debugging features and external tools like GDB, LLDB, and `perf`, you can effectively identify and resolve issues. Profiling helps uncover performance bottlenecks, and Zig's flexibility enables you to implement optimized solutions, whether through better algorithms, efficient memory management, or parallelism. Armed with these tools and techniques, you're well-equipped to write fast, robust Zig applications.

14. WRITING CROSS-PLATFORM CODE

One of the strengths of Zig is its emphasis on portability and cross-platform development. With its powerful compiler and minimal runtime, Zig makes it straightforward to write code that works seamlessly across multiple platforms. This capability is especially useful for applications that need to run on diverse environments like Linux, Windows, macOS, and even embedded systems.

In this discussion, we'll explore how to handle platform differences and utilize conditional compilation to write clean, cross-platform Zig code.

Why Cross-Platform Code Matters

Cross-platform code allows your application to reach a broader audience, reduce duplication of effort, and maintain consistency in behavior across environments. However, achieving this requires careful attention to platform-specific quirks, system calls, file systems, and libraries. Zig provides tools to manage these differences effectively without overwhelming complexity.

HANDLING PLATFORM DIFFERENCES

Platform differences may arise due to variations in file systems, networking APIs, or operating system behaviors. Zig handles these challenges with:

The `os` Module

The Zig standard library provides an `os` module, which abstracts platform-specific functionality like file I/O, process management, and system information.

Example: Reading a file in a cross-platform way:

```zig
const std = @import("std");

pub fn main() !void {
    const allocator = std.heap.page_allocator;

    // Cross-platform file read
    const file_path = "example.txt";
    const file = try std.fs.cwd().openFile(file_path, .{});
    defer file.close();

    const file_contents = try file.readAllAlloc(allocator);
    defer allocator.free(file_contents);

    std.debug.print("File contents: {s}\n", .{file_contents});
}
```

1. This code works across all supported platforms by leveraging Zig's os module to handle file operations.

Path Management

File path separators (/ vs. \) differ between Unix-like systems and Windows. Use Zig's path manipulation utilities to handle these automatically:

```
const std = @import("std");


pub fn main() void {

    const path = std.fs.path.join(std.heap.c_allocator,
"folder", "file.txt");

    std.debug.print("Platform-independent path: {s}\n",
.{path});

}
```

2. **Platform-Specific Features**
   If you need platform-specific functionality, Zig allows direct
   access to system APIs. For example:

On Windows:

```
const std = @import("std");


if (std.os.windows) {

    const kernel32 = @cImport(@cInclude("windows.h"));
```

```
        kernel32.MessageBoxA(null,  "Hello,  Windows!",
"Greetings", 0);
}
```

On Linux:

```
 const std = @import("std");
```

```
if (std.os.linux) {
    const libc = @cImport(@cInclude("unistd.h"));
    libc.write(1, "Hello, Linux!\n", 14);
}
```

CONDITIONAL COMPILATION

Zig's conditional compilation makes it easy to include or exclude code based on the target platform, architecture, or other build-time parameters.

Using `@import("builtin")` for Platform Information
 Zig provides the `@import("builtin")` function, which gives access to target-specific details like OS, architecture, and environment.

```
const builtin = @import("builtin");
```

```
pub fn main() void {

    if (builtin.os.tag == .windows) {

        std.debug.print("Running on Windows\n", .{});

    } else if (builtin.os.tag == .linux) {

        std.debug.print("Running on Linux\n", .{});

    } else {

            std.debug.print("Running  on  an  unsupported
platform\n", .{});

    }

}
```

This dynamically adjusts behavior based on the target operating system.

Compile-time Conditionals

For more granular control, use comptime to evaluate conditions during compilation:

```
pub fn platformSpecificFunction() void {

    comptime {
```

```
        if (@import("builtin").os.tag == .macos) {

            std.debug.print("macOS-specific code\n",
.{});

            } else if (@import("builtin").os.tag ==
.windows) {

            std.debug.print("Windows-specific code\n",
.{});

        }

    }

}
```

Since these conditions are resolved at compile time, they don't affect runtime performance.

Target-specific Files

If your project has large sections of platform-specific code, you can organize them into separate files and conditionally include them:

```
const platform = @import("platform");


pub fn main() void {

    platform.run();

}
```

```
platform.zig includes:

 const builtin = @import("builtin");


comptime {

    if (builtin.os.tag == .windows) {

                              pub    const    run    =
@import("windows_code.zig").run;

    } else if (builtin.os.tag == .linux) {

        pub const run = @import("linux_code.zig").run;

    }

}
```

1. This approach keeps platform-specific logic isolated, improving readability and maintainability.

Example: Cross-Platform File Monitor

Let's build a simple cross-platform file monitoring tool using conditional compilation.

Setup:
Create a Zig project and organize it like this:

```
src/
  main.zig
  monitor/
    linux.zig
    windows.zig
```

Main Code (`main.zig`):

```
const std = @import("std");
const monitor = @import("monitor");


pub fn main() !void {
    try monitor.watch("example.txt");
}
```

Linux Monitor (`linux.zig`):

```
const std = @import("std");


pub fn watch(file_path: []const u8) !void {
    const libc = @cImport(@cInclude("sys/inotify.h"));
    const fd = libc.inotify_init1(0);
```

```zig
    if (fd < 0) return error.FailedToInitialize;

    defer std.os.close(fd);

        const   wd   =   libc.inotify_add_watch(fd,
file_path.ptr, libc.IN_MODIFY);

    if (wd < 0) return error.FailedToAddWatch;

    var buffer: [1024]u8 = undefined;

    _ = std.os.read(fd, &buffer);

        std.debug.print("File   modified:   {s}\n",
.{file_path});

}
```

Windows Monitor (`windows.zig`):

```zig
const std = @import("std");

pub fn watch(file_path: []const u8) !void {
    const kernel32 = @cImport(@cInclude("windows.h"));

    const handle = kernel32.CreateFileA(

        file_path.ptr,

        0x00100000, // FILE_LIST_DIRECTORY
```

```zig
        0, null, 3, 0x02000000, null,
    );
    if (handle == null) return error.FailedToOpenFile;

    defer kernel32.CloseHandle(handle);

    var buffer: [1024]u8 = undefined;
    var bytesReturned: u32 = 0;

    kernel32.ReadDirectoryChangesW(
        handle, &buffer, @sizeOf(buffer), false,
        0x00000010, // FILE_NOTIFY_CHANGE_LAST_WRITE
        &bytesReturned, null, null,
    );
            std.debug.print("File   modified:   {s}\n",
.{file_path});
}
```

Platform Inclusion in `monitor.zig`:
```zig
const builtin = @import("builtin");
```

```
comptime {

    if (builtin.os.tag == .linux) {

        pub const watch = @import("linux.zig").watch;

    } else if (builtin.os.tag == .windows) {

        pub const watch = @import("windows.zig").watch;

    }

}
```

Zig's emphasis on explicit control and clarity makes it a powerful tool for writing cross-platform applications. By leveraging the os module, conditional compilation, and external platform APIs, you can handle platform differences elegantly while keeping your code maintainable. This flexibility ensures that your application runs consistently across environments without sacrificing performance or reliability. With these techniques, you're well-equipped to build robust, cross-platform Zig applications.

15. CONTRIBUTING TO ZIG PROJECTS

The Zig programming language has a vibrant and rapidly growing community of developers. Whether you're improving the language itself, contributing to libraries, or building tools for the ecosystem, contributing to Zig projects is a rewarding way to give back to the community, learn more about the language, and gain valuable open-source experience. In this discussion, we'll explore the Zig ecosystem, how you can get involved, and best practices for making meaningful contributions.

Zig Ecosystem Overview

The Zig ecosystem is diverse, encompassing the core language, official tools, and a variety of community-driven projects. Understanding its structure is the first step to contributing effectively.

1. **The Zig Language and Compiler**
    At the heart of the ecosystem is the Zig compiler and standard library. Hosted on GitHub, the Zig repository includes:
    - The Zig compiler, written in Zig and C++.
    - The standard library, which provides essential utilities for systems programming.
    - Documentation and test cases.
2. Contributions to the compiler often focus on bug fixes, optimizations, new language features, and improvements to tooling like `zig build`.

3. **Official Tools and Extensions**
    Zig also includes official tools like:

- zig fmt: A code formatter to ensure consistent style.
- zig build: A build system for Zig projects.
- zig test: A testing framework for validating code.
4. Enhancing these tools or creating additional utilities is another valuable way to contribute.

5. **Community Projects**
   Zig's community actively develops libraries, frameworks, and tools. Notable examples include:

   - **zls (Zig Language Server)**: Provides editor support for Zig.
   - **Mach**: A game engine built using Zig.
   - **zigmod**: A package manager for Zig projects.
6. These projects often welcome contributions ranging from feature development to documentation and issue triaging.

7. **Documentation and Learning Resources**
   Improving documentation, writing tutorials, and creating educational content are critical to helping new developers adopt Zig.

Getting Started with Contributing

Contributing to an open-source project can seem intimidating, but the Zig community is welcoming and encourages collaboration.

1. **Familiarize Yourself with Zig**
   Before contributing, spend time learning Zig by:

   - Reading the official documentation.
   - Exploring the standard library and its modules.

- Building small projects to understand Zig's design philosophy.

2. **Choose a Project**

   Identify a project aligned with your interests and skills. If you're new, start with community-driven projects or documentation improvements, as they often have simpler tasks.

Find Issues to Work On

Many repositories label beginner-friendly issues. Look for tags like good first issue or help wanted. For example, the Zig GitHub repository includes these labels to guide new contributors.

Example: To find such issues, run:

is:open label:"good first issue" repo:ziglang/zig

3.

Clone and Build the Project

Before making changes, clone and build the project to familiarize yourself with its structure. For the Zig compiler:

```
git clone https://github.com/ziglang/zig.git

cd zig

build/zig build
```

This builds the Zig compiler from source. Run tests to ensure the build is successful:

```
build/zig test
```

4. **Make Contributions**

   ○ Start with small, manageable tasks.
   ○ Follow the project's contribution guidelines, typically documented in `CONTRIBUTING.md`.

5. **Submit a Pull Request (PR)**
   When ready, submit your changes via a PR. Be sure to:

   ○ Clearly describe the issue being addressed.
   ○ Reference related issues or discussions.
   ○ Ensure your code passes all tests.

Best Practices for Contributing

To make meaningful and effective contributions, follow these best practices:

1. **Understand Zig's Philosophy**
   Zig prioritizes simplicity, explicitness, and performance. When contributing, adhere to these principles. Avoid introducing unnecessary abstractions or features that conflict with Zig's minimalist approach.

Follow Code Style and Guidelines

Zig enforces a consistent code style using `zig fmt`. Run it before submitting changes:

```
zig fmt path/to/file.zig
```

2. This ensures your code adheres to the project's standards.

Write Tests for Your Changes

Zig emphasizes testing as part of the development process. Add tests to validate your changes and avoid regressions.

Example: Adding a test for a new function in the standard library:

```
test "example test" {

    const result = someFunction();

    try std.testing.expect(result == expectedValue);

}
```

3. **Communicate Effectively**
   Engage with the maintainers and community by:

   - Participating in discussions on GitHub issues or forums.
   - Providing clear commit messages and PR descriptions.
   - Being respectful and open to feedback.

4. **Document Your Work**
   If you add new features or APIs, update the documentation to reflect your changes. Clear documentation helps others understand and use your contributions.

5. **Stay Active in the Community**
   Contributing goes beyond code. Attend Zig-related meetups, join the Zig Discord, or participate in mailing lists to stay connected with the community.

6.

Example: Contributing to the Zig Compiler

Let's walk through an example of contributing to Zig's compiler. Suppose there's an issue labeled good first issue that requests better error messages for invalid array indexing.

1. **Understand the Problem**
   Review the issue description and understand how the compiler currently handles invalid indexing. Reproduce the error locally to observe its behavior.

2. **Locate the Relevant Code**
   In the Zig compiler source, the file responsible for array indexing might be in src/. Use search tools to identify relevant functions, such as analyzeArrayIndex.

Make the Changes
Enhance the error message:

```
const std = @import("std");



fn analyzeArrayIndex(index: usize, array: []const u8)
void {

    if (index >= array.len) {

            @panic("Index out of bounds: index={} is
greater than or equal to array length={}", .{index,
array.len});

    }
```

```
}
```

Test the Changes

Add a test case to verify the new behavior:

```zig
test "index out of bounds error" {
    const array = [_]u8{1, 2, 3};
    try std.testing.expectPanic(@panic("Index out of
bounds"), fn () void {
        _ = array[5];
    });
}
```

3. **Submit a PR**

   Commit your changes, push them to your fork, and open a pull request. In your PR description:

   ○ Explain the issue.
   ○ Describe your solution.
   ○ Include the test case and results.

Contributing to Zig projects is an excellent way to deepen your understanding of the language and help shape its future. By familiarizing yourself with the ecosystem, engaging with the community, and adhering to best practices, you can make meaningful contributions that benefit everyone. Whether you're fixing bugs, writing documentation, or creating libraries, your efforts will be appreciated and impactful.

Part 4:
CASE STUDIES AND NEXT STEPS

CASE STUDIES AND NEXT STEPS

This section of *Hands-On Zig Programming* takes you beyond the foundational concepts and practical applications covered earlier, guiding you into real-world scenarios and future opportunities. It is designed to demonstrate the potential of Zig through carefully selected case studies and to equip you with the knowledge and inspiration needed to continue your Zig programming journey.

Programming is most rewarding when theoretical understanding is paired with hands-on problem-solving. In this part, we'll dive into case studies that showcase how Zig is applied to solve real-world challenges. These examples are drawn from diverse domains, including systems programming, performance-critical libraries, and cross-platform tools. By analyzing these projects, you'll gain insights into the design choices, patterns, and optimizations that make Zig an outstanding language for practical use cases.

Each case study is more than a mere walkthrough; it is an opportunity to explore the thought processes behind designing and implementing solutions in Zig. We'll dissect the architecture, highlight key features of the language that were utilized, and discuss how Zig's unique properties—such as explicitness, performance, and safety—contribute to the success of the application.

After the case studies, we shift our focus to the future. Whether you're a professional developer looking to adopt Zig for enterprise-grade applications, an enthusiast experimenting with open-source contributions, or a student seeking to deepen your skills, this section will provide actionable steps to guide you. Topics include exploring advanced Zig features, engaging with the Zig community, contributing to ecosystem projects, and preparing for upcoming trends in systems programming.

By the end of this section, you'll have a clear vision of how to leverage Zig for your projects and how to stay at the forefront of its evolving ecosystem. The goal is not just to solidify your knowledge but to inspire you to push the boundaries of what's possible with Zig.

15. CASE STUDY: BUILDING A COMPLETE APPLICATION

In this case study, we will walk through building a complete, end-to-end Zig application. The objective of this case study is to demonstrate Zig's capabilities in constructing a functional, cross-platform CLI application from start to finish. The project we'll build is a **Task Manager CLI tool**, which allows users to add, view, and delete tasks from the command line. By walking through this case study, you'll gain a comprehensive understanding of various concepts such as file operations, argument parsing, system interactions, and best practices for building robust applications in Zig.

Let's explore everything step by step.

Project Overview

Our goal is to create a simple but functional CLI application that allows users to manage tasks. Here's what we want the Task Manager CLI to do:

- Add tasks
- List existing tasks
- Delete tasks
- Save tasks to disk and reload them on startup

We'll use the command line interface to interact with the application. The primary goal of this project is to show how you can combine various Zig features, such as file I/O, argument parsing, and system interactions, into a cohesive, well-structured project.

Step 1: Setting Up the Project

Before we dive in, let's set up our project structure. Your project directory might look like this:

```
task-manager/
├── src/
│   ├── main.zig
│   ├── tasks.zig
│   ├── storage.zig
├── build.zig
└── task-manager.zig
```

- `src/main.zig`: Entry point of the CLI application.
- `src/tasks.zig`: Module to manage tasks in memory and provide operations.
- `src/storage.zig`: Handles storing tasks to disk and loading them.
- `build.zig`: Build script for compiling the project.
- `task-manager.zig`: Configuration and main project setup.

Step 2: Initial Project Configuration

We begin by setting up our build script. The `build.zig` script tells the Zig compiler how to build our application.

Here's a simple `build.zig`:

const Builder = @import("std").build.Builder;

```
pub fn build(b: *Builder) void {
    const mode = b.args.mode();
        const exe = b.addExecutable("task-manager",
"src/main.zig");
    exe.setBuildMode(mode);
    exe.setTarget(b.target);
```

```
    b.installArtifact(exe);
}
```

This build script compiles `src/main.zig` into a CLI executable named `task-manager`.

Step 3: Define the Task Structure

Our CLI application needs to handle tasks in memory first before persisting them. Let's create the `tasks.zig` file to represent this functionality.

src/tasks.zig

```
const std = @import("std");


pub const Task = struct {
    id: u32,

    description: []const u8,

    completed: bool,
};



pub fn create_task(task_list: *[]Task, description: []const u8) void {
    const id = task_list.len + 1;
```

```
    task_list.* = task_list.++(Task{id, description,
false});

            std.debug.print("Task    added:    {s}\n",
.{description});

}


pub fn list_tasks(task_list: []Task) void {

    if (task_list.len == 0) {

            std.debug.print("No  tasks  currently
present.\n", .{});

        return;

    }

    for (task_list) |task| {

        const status = if (task.completed) "completed"
else "pending";

        std.debug.print("{d}. {s} - {s}\n", .{task.id,
task.description, status});

    }

}


pub fn delete_task(task_list: *[]Task, id: u32) void {
```

```zig
    var i: usize = 0;

    while (i < task_list.len) {

        if (task_list[i].id == id) {

            task_list.* = std.mem.splice(task_list, i,
1);

                std.debug.print("Task {d} removed.\n",
.{id});

            return;

        }

        i += 1;

    }

    std.debug.print("Task {d} not found.\n", .{id});

}
```

This module manages tasks in memory, allowing us to add, list, and delete tasks. Tasks have an id, a description, and a completed status. This modular design lets us encapsulate our business logic independently.

Step 4: Persistent Storage Integration

Now that we have in-memory task management, let's persist our tasks to disk using simple JSON serialization.

src/storage.zig

```zig
const std = @import("std");
```

```
fn save_tasks(path: []const u8, tasks: []Task) !void {

    const file = try std.fs.cwd().openFile(path, .{
.write = true });

    defer file.close();


    const data = std.fmt.bufAlloc(100, "{d}\n",
.{tasks});

    try file.writeAll(data);

    std.debug.print("Tasks saved to disk\n", .{});

}


fn load_tasks(path: []const u8) []Task {

    var tasks = []Task{};

    if (try std.fs.cwd().exists(path)) {

        const file_contents = try
std.fs.cwd().readFile(path);

        tasks = std.mem.split(file_contents, '\n');

        return tasks;

    }

    return tasks;
```

```
}
```

In `src/storage.zig`, we've demonstrated saving tasks to disk and reading them back. Zig's built-in file I/O operations seamlessly interact with the OS-level interfaces to manage disk storage.

Conclusion

Building the Task Manager CLI project in Zig illustrates several important practical programming concepts. We explored CLI interface interactions, persistent storage integration, and platform compatibility.

- **CLI Integration** showcased Zig's argument parsing and system command interface.
- **Task Persistence to Disk** demonstrated our ability to serialize data, manage files, and optimize memory interactions.
- **End-to-End Modular Design** revealed Zig's commitment to simplicity, performance, and explicit programming style, allowing concise yet maintainable code structures.

Working on this project gave you foundational experience with Zig's strengths: speed, safety, cross-platform compatibility, and performance. Whether you continue improving CLI tools, work on system-level projects, or explore Zig's community modules, this experience will solidly ground your real-world application development skills.

17. THE ZIG ECOSYSTEM AND COMMUNITY

As you grow more familiar with Zig, understanding its ecosystem and community becomes increasingly important. The Zig programming language is not just a standalone tool—it is part of a larger ecosystem of libraries, tools, contributors, and community interactions. Knowing how to engage with the ecosystem, leverage existing libraries, and stay connected to ongoing developments will enable you to build robust, scalable applications while contributing back to the community. In this section, we'll explore the various aspects of the Zig ecosystem, highlight useful libraries and tools, and discuss ways to stay informed and actively involved with the Zig community.

EXPLORING ZIG LIBRARIES AND TOOLS

Zig has a growing ecosystem that includes libraries, tools, and utilities built by the community and official Zig contributors. Let's break down the key areas where you'll find useful resources and how to navigate the ecosystem to get the most out of it.

The Standard Library

The Zig standard library is a robust and well-maintained collection of utilities and tools essential for most systems programming tasks. The standard library includes everything from string manipulation and memory operations to file I/O and networking.

- **File I/O**
  The standard library provides comprehensive support for reading from and writing to files. Operations are performed with low overhead and high performance.
- **Memory Management**
  Zig's memory model prioritizes safety and performance, and the standard library provides explicit memory operations that avoid

the pitfalls of garbage collection. Functions for dynamic memory allocation, stack allocation, and pointer arithmetic are all part of the core utilities

- **Networking Utilities**
  Networking operations such as sockets, HTTP requests, and inter-process communication are well integrated in the Zig standard library. This allows you to build networked applications with a clean and straightforward syntax.
- **String Manipulation and Formatting**
  String operations in Zig are simple and efficient. The standard library includes functions for formatting, concatenation, splitting, and searching through strings.

Third-Party Libraries

The Zig ecosystem also contains a growing number of community-developed libraries and tools. These projects offer additional functionalities and can help extend the standard library's capabilities in areas where specialized support is needed. Here are a few popular community contributions:

ZigMod

ZigMod acts as a package manager and dependency management tool for Zig projects. It simplifies the process of adding third-party libraries to your project and managing versioning.

How to Use ZigMod:
Install ZigMod via:

zigmod init

- Then, add dependencies to your project configuration, and ZigMod will handle fetching and linking them automatically.

- **ZLS (Zig Language Server)**
  ZLS enhances the developer experience by integrating with popular editors (VS Code, Sublime Text, etc.) and providing features such as syntax highlighting, error detection, and code completion. Installing ZLS makes it easier to work with Zig codebases.

- **Zig Game Engines and Frameworks**
  Several projects have adapted Zig for game development and multimedia applications, like **Mach**, a simple and performant game engine. Such projects demonstrate Zig's potential in performance-intensive domains.

Build Tools

Zig's build tools reflect its commitment to simplicity and performance:

`zig build`
The Zig compiler itself includes a robust build system integrated with the `zig build` command. It is designed to be fast and efficient while allowing you to define complex build configurations.

Here's a basic example:

zig build run

-

Cross-Compilation
Zig is known for its cross-compilation capabilities, which let you

compile code for different operating systems (Windows, macOS, Linux) and architectures effortlessly.

To build your project for a different target system:
```
zig    build-exe    main.zig    --target-os    windows
--target-arch x86_64
```

Debugging and Profiling Tools

Zig offers robust debugging and profiling tools integrated with the standard compiler:

- **Built-in Debugging Support**
  With Zig, you have direct access to debug symbols and can debug applications using GDB or built-in log outputs. You can also use Zig's diagnostic tools to check memory and runtime performance.
- **Profiling Utilities**
  Profiling Zig applications helps identify bottlenecks. Zig has built-in profiling commands that you can use to measure runtime performance and memory consumption, ensuring high efficiency and low overhead in production-grade applications.

STAYING UPDATED WITH ZIG'S DEVELOPMENT

The Zig ecosystem is continuously evolving, with frequent updates and contributions from both the core Zig team and the community. Staying current with developments will help you maintain best practices, utilize new features, and contribute effectively to ongoing projects.

Official Resources

- **The Official Website**
  The Zig programming language's official website (ziglang.org) is

the central hub for documentation, updates, and news. It contains detailed sections about getting started, core features, language reference, and tutorials.

- **GitHub Repository**
  The core development of Zig happens on its GitHub repository: https://github.com/ziglang/zig
  Here, you can find source code, commit history, active pull requests, and detailed issues. You'll also find discussions about proposed changes and enhancements.

- **Community Forums**
  The Zig community thrives in forums and chat groups. You can find valuable interactions, tips, and discussions in:

  - The **Zig Discord Server**
  - Reddit communities dedicated to Zig
  - Various developer forums and chat groups where Zig contributors collaborate

Social Media and Communication Channels

- **Twitter**
  Many core developers and community members share updates, news, and interesting Zig developments on Twitter. Following prominent developers will keep you in the loop about new releases and updates.

- **Newsletters and Blogs**
  The Zig community often publishes blogs and newsletters that summarize updates, new features, and contributions. Subscribe to newsletters like the Zig Weekly Digest to get regular updates

delivered directly to your inbox.

- **YouTube Tutorials and Talks**
  Several developers share tutorials, conference talks, and
  workshops on platforms like YouTube. These resources often
  include deeper dives into specific topics such as performance
  optimization, debugging, and project best practices.

Contributing to the Community

Engaging with the Zig community is a mutually beneficial way to learn
and contribute. Here's how you can get involved:

1. **Submit Pull Requests**
   Many open issues on the Zig GitHub repository are open for
   contributions. Even if you contribute a small bug fix or improve
   the documentation, it helps maintain the ecosystem's robustness
   and usability.

2. **Answer Questions and Participate in Discussions**
   Help others by answering questions on forums like Reddit, Stack
   Overflow, or Zig chat groups. Engaging in discussions and sharing
   insights not only helps others but also strengthens your
   understanding of the language.

3. **Write Tutorials and Create Content**
   Sharing your knowledge through tutorials, blog posts, or video
   content can help new developers learn Zig faster. Additionally, it
   provides opportunities to showcase your own projects and
   expertise.

4. **Collaborate on Open-Source Projects**
   Many open-source projects use Zig for different purposes—from system tools to game engines. Contributing to these projects can teach you advanced Zig programming techniques and best practices.

The Zig ecosystem and community offer an abundance of resources and opportunities for developers at all levels. The strength of the Zig ecosystem lies not only in its performance and simplicity but also in the collaborative efforts of its community members and contributors. Whether you're utilizing the built-in tools and libraries, exploring third-party libraries, or contributing to open-source projects, there's always a chance to learn, optimize, and contribute.

Being active in the Zig community, following ongoing developments, and continuously contributing to projects will help you grow as a developer while supporting the evolution of Zig as a performant and versatile language. As the ecosystem expands and more developers adopt Zig for production projects, you will find yourself not just using Zig but shaping its future direction—an experience that is both fulfilling and professionally enriching.

Conclusion

Congratulations on reaching the end of *Hands-on Zig Programming: A Practical Guide to Building Real-World Systems Applications for Developers*! You've taken an important step in your journey as a developer, mastering a language that emphasizes performance, simplicity, and low-level control while being accessible and practical. Zig offers a unique combination of power, clarity, and performance that makes it a standout choice for building real-world systems applications. In this book, we've explored the ins and outs of Zig, from the basics to more advanced concepts, and delved into practical examples that demonstrated its capabilities in real-world scenarios. Let's reflect on what you've learned, where you can go from here, and how you can continue to grow your knowledge and contributions to the Zig ecosystem.

Understanding Zig: A Strong Foundation

By now, you should have a solid foundation in Zig's core concepts. Zig is not just another programming language; it's a tool that bridges the gap between high-level abstraction and low-level control. You've seen how Zig prioritizes performance without compromising readability. Whether you've been working with low-level system calls, memory management, or networking interfaces, you've learned that Zig provides developers with complete transparency and control over what happens under the hood.

Zig's commitment to simplicity and correctness means that you don't have to deal with the unnecessary complexities that some other languages bring. Instead, you have explicit memory control, a clear and concise syntax, and powerful tools for cross-compilation, debugging, and profiling.

Key Takeaways from the Book

Let's recap some key concepts that have been covered throughout the book, ensuring you have a clear mental map of the Zig landscape.

1. **Core Concepts and Syntax**
   You've grasped the essentials of Zig's syntax, its strong typing system, and the simplicity that comes with minimalistic language design. These basics serve as the building blocks for everything else you'll do with Zig. The explicitness of Zig's syntax and operations avoids ambiguity, making your code self-documenting and maintainable.

2. **Building Real-World Applications**
   The chapter on building real-world applications showed you how Zig is a powerful tool for creating production-level software. From CLI tools to system utilities, you've seen how to structure, test, and optimize applications in a clean and scalable way. You've learned to navigate dependencies, handle inputs and outputs, and interact with the operating system effectively.

3. **Networking and Concurrency**
   Networking and concurrency are crucial for real-world applications, and you've seen how Zig handles these areas with low-level control and high efficiency. Whether you were setting up sockets, managing protocols, or ensuring thread safety and performance, you explored key strategies to build scalable and robust networked applications.

4. **Optimization and Performance**
   Performance optimization was a key theme throughout this book. You've explored custom allocators, memory profiling, and

debugging tools that give you granular control over your system's resources. This allows you to create software that doesn't just work but is fast, efficient, and scalable.

5. **Interoperability with C and Other Languages**
   Zig's interoperability with C is a standout feature that opens up many possibilities. Whether you were linking C libraries, wrapping legacy code, or integrating third-party solutions, you saw how Zig allows seamless integration while maintaining performance.

6. **Cross-Platform Development**
   Another significant benefit of using Zig is its ability to target multiple platforms with ease. The lessons on cross-compilation and platform-specific code paths highlighted how you can build software that runs smoothly on Windows, macOS, and Linux without duplicating efforts or compromising performance.

7. **Debugging and Profiling**
   Debugging and profiling are essential skills for any developer, and Zig offers a toolkit that integrates these capabilities directly into the development process. You've learned to diagnose performance issues, manage memory efficiently, and fine-tune applications for optimal performance.

8. **The Zig Community and Ecosystem**
   We've seen that Zig is not just a language but a vibrant ecosystem with a growing community. Open-source projects, community forums, libraries, and tools are all places where you can learn, contribute, and grow. Engaging with the community provides support, collaboration, and opportunities to contribute back to

open-source projects, allowing you to refine your skills and help others along the way.

Where Do You Go from Here?

Now that you have a solid understanding of Zig and how to use it in real-world applications, the next step is to deepen your knowledge and put your skills to work in bigger and more challenging projects. Here are some actionable steps you can take:

Contribute to Open-Source Projects

Contributing to open-source projects is a fantastic way to get more hands-on experience. Many open-source projects are written in Zig, and you can find opportunities to contribute to libraries, fix bugs, optimize code, and add new features. Not only will this improve your coding skills, but you'll also become part of the growing Zig community.

Look for projects on platforms like GitHub, contribute pull requests, and actively engage in code reviews. Participate in discussions, propose improvements, and learn from the feedback provided by other experienced developers.

Build More Complex Applications

Now that you have the fundamentals, try building more complex and scalable applications. Consider projects like:

- **Distributed Systems:** Implement a distributed file system or a distributed database to understand network protocols, concurrency, and system performance optimization.
- **CLI Tools:** Develop CLI tools for data processing, monitoring, and automation, showcasing Zig's ability to create lightweight and efficient system utilities.

- **Embedded Systems:** Explore embedded programming and create applications for microcontrollers, focusing on performance and resource constraints.

Master Memory Management

Memory management is a fundamental area where Zig excels. Take time to experiment with custom allocators, memory pools, and different allocation strategies. Analyze memory leaks, optimize memory access patterns, and explore performance profiling tools to get insights into how your applications use system resources.

Explore Compiler Internals

Zig's compiler is a powerful tool that you can customize and extend. Study the compiler internals to understand how it optimizes code and performs cross-compilation. Try modifying or extending the compiler behavior to learn how low-level systems interactions work. This deeper knowledge will make you a better systems programmer and improve your overall performance optimization skills.

Cross-Platform Testing

Ensure that your projects run smoothly across different operating systems and architectures. Use Zig's cross-compilation features to build applications on one platform and run them on others. Set up automated testing workflows to verify cross-platform compatibility, ensuring that your code remains robust and bug-free.

Stay Active in the Zig Community

Being active in the Zig community will help you stay up to date with the latest developments. Participate in community discussions, attend meetups and conferences, and contribute to forums. Follow core developers on social media, join the Zig Discord channel, and contribute to forums like Reddit or Stack Overflow.

Sharing your knowledge, asking questions, and mentoring new developers not only strengthens your expertise but also helps grow the Zig community as a whole. The more active the community, the better the ecosystem becomes, with more tools, libraries, and collaborative opportunities.

Final Thoughts

As we close this book, remember that Zig is not just a programming language; it's a tool that empowers you with control, performance, and clarity. Whether you're building operating systems, working on networking tools, creating embedded applications, or contributing to open-source projects, Zig offers an unparalleled combination of performance and simplicity.

The journey of mastering Zig is ongoing. The landscape of software development is constantly evolving, and Zig's ecosystem is growing alongside it. As new contributors join the community, as new features are added to the language, and as new projects emerge, you'll find opportunities to learn, contribute, and grow.

Your path as a Zig developer is not just about writing efficient code—it's about being part of a community that values performance, simplicity, and transparency. Continue experimenting, keep learning, and share your knowledge with others. Build, optimize, debug, and contribute—push boundaries and explore new ideas. By doing so, you'll not only enhance your skills but also contribute to the development and success of the Zig language and ecosystem.

Thank you for taking this journey through *Hands-on Zig Programming*. We hope you leave this book with a deeper understanding of Zig's strengths, a toolkit full of practical knowledge, and a network of connections within the community. The road ahead is filled with challenges and opportunities, and now you're equipped with a language and a community that supports your growth as a developer.

Keep building, keep learning, and continue to push the boundaries of what Zig can do. The future of Zig is bright, and with your continued curiosity and commitment, you'll play an important role in shaping that future.

www.ingramcontent.com/pod-product-compliance
Lightning Source LLC
Chambersburg PA
CBHW071156050326
40689CB00011B/2133